33 QUESTIONS TO ASK BEFORE YOUR 3RD DATE

Things you must know to avoid wasting your time

DR. TAMILORE ODIMAYO PSYD

Website www.MentalHealthSavage.org

First Edition: 2025

ISBN-13: 979-8-9998518-1-9

Printed in the United States of America

Other Books by Tamilore Odimayo

Olivetti: Inception

Olivetti: Illumination

Olivetti: Inferno

Game of Confessions

Cheat Code

Relationship Code

How to be a Mental Health Savage

Diary of a Psychopath

This book is for my mother. Watching you offer family planning counseling over the years inspired me to choose my career path.

TABLE OF CONTENTS

FOREWORD

The most important decision you will ever make is who you choose to form a sexual relationship with. It determines what trauma, medical illnesses, behaviors, wealth, culture, and religion will be passed down to the next generation. Despite this, people enter sexual relationships without considering the risks and act like there is unlimited time in the dating game. Charles Darwin—yes, that guy who believed we evolved from monkeys—famously said, "A man who dares to waste one hour has not discovered the value of life.

Let me put this into perspective. Life expectancy in the United States is 77 years. The average person spends about 18 years under the care and supervision of their parents, leaving roughly 59 years for adulthood and decision-making. Here's where it gets interesting. In this short period, you're expected to find a career, start it, hope it goes well enough to start a family, find a partner, possibly buy a house, raise children, work, ensure your children don't become a menace to society, retire, raise your grandchildren, and wait for time to pass. For women, only 32 years of those 59 are available for procreation. Scientifically, just 17 of those years are viable to avoid a geriatric pregnancy. Even more time is wasted during those 17 viable years. Many people start casually and only become serious after their mid-twenties, which leaves them with even less time to find a suitable partner. Before you know it, you're thirty-three years old, scrambling to make the most of what's left in the dating game. Not ideal!

When I work with individuals who have recently experienced a long-term breakup or divorce, I am often surprised by the limited information they possess about their partners before marrying or dating. I understand; recent research shows that 70% of individuals are meeting their future loved ones online, and this online world is a perfect venue for deception. Consequently, most individuals fall for the façade rather than reality. In my book, "How to Be a Mental Health Savage," I discuss the dangers of being anything other than yourself. Wearing a mask attracts people who are drawn to the mask and not to you. In this book, I will discuss key questions you need to ask to master the dating game.

In the medieval period, courtship was as quick as a bullet train because life expectancy was dangerously low. Your family would seek out a suitable partner with an impressive family name; they would introduce you, and you would spend time walking around the garden (supervised, of course. It would be a tragedy if a woman's virtue were questioned). If things went well and the chemistry was right, you would tie the knot. Before all this, a wealthy bachelor or spinster would have several suitors and feel compelled to court multiple individuals until they found the right one. This courtship period did not last months or years; in some cases, it lasted only days or weeks.

I understand. In today's world, it's unrealistic to expect otherwise. No one wants to rush into a life-changing decision. And, oh, the increased life expectancy and medical advancements mean we can afford to take our time. Back then, life expectancy was typically in the mid-thirties to mid-forties. Two teenagers would have been paired because birth factors needed to be taken into consideration. The older a woman was, the higher the risk of pregnancy, especially given the limited medical resources. So, everything had to be done quickly: marriage, children, and the constant threat of war or plague that could wipe them out before they reached forty.

Currently, in some African, Asian, and Indian tribes, arranged marriages are still part of life and help individuals reduce the courtship period significantly. One of my closest friends from the Igbo tribe in Nigeria told me that her parents, who had been married for thirty years, only knew each other for a week before getting married. I gasped at the thought of that. Before you jump to conclusions, this book will not teach you how to find "the one" in a week. Her tribe could do this because it was a collective society where families knew each other and their histories. In most individualistic societies, where information is often based on false stories on platforms like TikTok, Facebook, Instagram, and Twitter, it's essential to double-check your potential partner so you don't waste your time. Again, I have mentioned "time" multiple times for a reason. Time waits for no one.

So, are you the person waiting for your partner to change? Are you the individual known for choosing the "Wrong" person? Are you blind to red flags? Are you having trouble seeing through the nonsense? Are you the one who senses something is off about a potential partner but can't quite put your finger on what it is? Are you five years into a relationship and still unsure if you should marry that person? Are you tired of the Tinder culture where people want to waste your time? If these questions apply to you, you're reading the right book. Although I'm a licensed clinician who strives to be polite in every way, I will be as honest as possible. So, get ready, and let me show you how to avoid wasting your time.

For the best results, you don't need to ask your potential partner every question verbatim. However, it's important to keep these questions in mind during your first three dates to help identify potential red flags. For convenience, review the table of contents to find out which questions are most relevant to your current situation.

The basic knowledge of the Relationship Cycle

The relationship cycle isn't complicated. Many authors, writers, and social scientists use different definitions, but they convey the same concept.

There are four stages in the relationship cycle. The A.B.C.D. principle makes it easy to understand.

Awkward Stage

In the first stage, there is considerable uncertainty and awkwardness. You meet someone who attracts you and approach them. You begin to question whether you are responding to the right signals. Conversations feel uncomfortable, and dates can resemble a battlefield of uncertainty. You want to say and do the right thing as perfectly as you can.

At this stage, a significant amount of money is spent on impressing, ensuring that the outfits, restaurant choices, and event tickets are flawless. Individuals unconsciously defer honesty for later in the relationship due to personal skepticism. If you're at this stage, you find yourself trying to impress with gifts, planning additional date nights, and making greater efforts to establish your presence in your lover's life.

Here's the downside: the Awkward Stage is plagued by "masks," also known as pretense. This book will teach you how to break that habit in yourself and in the person with whom you are trying to establish a relationship. Why? If you wear a mask, you will attract people drawn to the mask, not to you. It's a simple principle. You will attract the right person when you present as your authentic self.

Bonding Stage

The first stage might last a while. Some couples never leave the first stage. Based on compatibility, if everything goes well, the second stage should reflect progress. Awkward conversations become less uncomfortable. By the time the first kiss happens, one doesn't need to worry about whether it's the right moment to kiss, touch, or even talk. Life becomes more fluid, and partner vulnerability increases.

This stage is the most appropriate time for sex to begin. Research shows that couples who have sex on the first date rarely make it long-term, but couples who have sex after getting to know one another tend to go much further than the average couple.

It is essential to address all the questions this book presents before proceeding to the next stage, as the sunk cost fallacy can arise when you reach the comfort stage. For those who are unfamiliar, the sunk cost fallacy is a phenomenon where a person is reluctant to leave a situation that is no longer working due to the investments already made. You don't want to invest too much in a relationship until you determine if it is worthwhile.

Comfort Stage

Never farted in front of your significant other before? Farts begin. Never burped? Yep, you feel more comfortable letting out what sounds like a hurricane from your mouth. At this stage, couples become comfortable and don't try as hard. Typically, the relationship is well-defined, and the daily routine becomes more regular. Sweatpants and gym shorts seem to be the go-to outfits. Both might have been introduced to parents and other family members by this stage. Sex becomes more consistent. Couples learn each other's likes, dislikes, wants, and needs. At this stage, most couples get married or move in together.

Disdain Stage

Some couples never reach this level of the relationship cycle. Some remain in the third level for the rest of their lives. In this stage, couples begin to argue about trivial matters, such as leaving dishes in the sink, not taking out the trash, farting, talking too much, talking too little, the amount of time spent together, and so on.

This stage is difficult because the initial attraction has faded. Romantic efforts wane due to a lack of interest or resentment, and the conflict seems endless. Some couples might feel they are missing out on other "fun" things and long for their single days. This may lead to feelings of intense isolation, grumbling, anger, and resentment. During this stage, infidelity is most likely to occur.

If a partner engages in infidelity, is caught, and is forgiven, the cycle of the relationship begins anew, starting from the awkward beginning and progressing through the subsequent stages. Hopefully, it will stop at the C stage next time.

Now that you understand the basics of the Relationship Cycle, let's delve into the intricate details of the types of people you will encounter while dating.

TYPES OF DATING PERSONALITIES

I narrowed down dating personalities based on the traits of people I have dated, people my clients have dated, and individuals I have observed on dating shows. Understanding a person's dating personality gives you an edge regarding the type of experience you will have throughout the relationship. To learn about your potential partner's dating personality, assessing who they are before telling them what you want in a relationship is essential.

When someone you like asks you, "What do you like in a person?" respond with, "While I would like to share that with you, what I want is best observed than told." This statement will automatically prevent you from being with someone who can pretend. I have heard people say during a post-breakup, marriage, or divorce counseling session, "In the beginning, it was all…" Yes, it would all be roses and diamonds because you either told them what you were looking for, they unconsciously guessed based on your personality, or the new car smell effect was actively in play. You need to look for consistency in how the individual acts under pressure. People operating from trauma will taste like lime when squeezed—bitter. People operating from love and healing will taste like oranges when squeezed—sweet. A person can only give from what is within. Stay tuned and learn about the types of Daters you will find.

THE RESCUER

"I only want to be in a relationship where I feel needed."

The Rescuer feels a strong responsibility for their potential partner's problems. They are good listeners, possess high levels of empathy, and often feel a need to "save" the world. Both genders often adopt this "rescue" role, but in different ways.

In some situations, the Rescuer needs to support their potential partner financially. For example, during a date, the person you're interested in complains about not having enough money or being between two jobs, and here you are, seeing the potential of a positive relationship, and then boom: Cash app/Venmo $500. In other situations, the Rescuer acts like a therapist by processing trauma, providing advice, helping their potential partner cope with life stressors, and more.

In my practice, I have observed that the core trait of the Rescuer is a tendency to people-please. People-pleasing is a condition in which a person is addicted to gaining favor from another individual at their own expense. The Rescuer also tends to attract the Victim, the Child, or the Desperate (explained later in this book).

Kyle, a middle-aged African American male, was always stuck in a financial rut, regardless of how much money he made. He consistently zeroed out his account before the end of his payday. A glorified Rescuer and People Pleaser, Kyle often wondered why every woman he attracted seemed to need him for something, despite their financial success. One day, Kyle came to my office complaining about his finances, and I asked him a series of questions that led me to his Facebook profile picture, which featured him posing in front of his bright blue Mustang with a wad of cash in both hands. When I asked Kyle why he was surprised that people always contacted him for money, he appeared confused. I explained that he presented what he had to offer to feel loved by his environment. Naturally, he would receive a thousand likes on those posts, but that attention also brought several women responding to his Direct Messages to tap into what he presented; he would offer.

Psychologically speaking, it is safe to say that Kyle's childhood was plagued by the belief that love is based on how much he can give to his environment. Kyle has relationships and friendships on payroll. Even if Kyle attempts to change his profile picture and image, he will always encounter someone with a financial need.

In every dating personality type in this book, the personality traits range from low to high. Jane, a medium Rescuer, struggled for years to accept her sexuality. After her father passed away, Jane decided to "come out" to her mother and began dating women. Within two months, Jane created a new identity but could not shake her core need to protect everyone from experiencing what she had. The first five women she dated were chronically depressed due to their family structure and their difficulty accepting their sexuality. Time and again, Jane became a therapist, mentor, doctor, and motivator. She felt that if she could guide these women through the traumas they experienced, they would be able to love her happily.

A rescuer usually thinks, "If my partner is happy, I'm happy." However, it takes time to understand that sometimes preventing a person from falling doesn't teach them how to get back up; if they don't know how to get back up, they will always depend on you.

If you need to rescue someone within the first few dates, ask why. Is there an underlying trauma that has not been resolved in your life? Is your need to rescue based on having an excess of what the person needs? That is, being in a great mental space to help address someone's traumatic experience or having more money than you can handle. Do you feel excessive guilt for problems you did not create? The answer to this question will determine whether you might end up in a codependent relationship.

RESCUER TEST

Questions below are rated on a scale from 1 to 5, with 5 indicating strong agreement and 1 indicating strong disagreement. A score of 3 is considered neutral. Add up your scores for each dating personality type. The answer with the highest score is most likely your dating personality type.

1. *It is vital for me to feel needed in a relationship.*
2. *I have a strong sense of responsibility for problems I did not cause.*
3. *It is difficult for me to say no to my partner*
4. *I feel excited about helping my partner with their problems, even when they don't need me.*
5. *I tend to be overly invested in helping my partner become who they aspire to be.*
6. *When my partner doesn't need me, I find myself looking for ways to foster a need.*
7. *I find it challenging to feel happy when my partner is unhappy.*
8. *I tend to feel bored or withdraw from my partner when I feel unneeded.*
9. *I am frequently referred to as a people pleaser.*
10. *I would rather suffer than let my partner suffer.*

TOTAL SCORE: _____

0-15 Low chance of being a Rescuer

15-30 Medium chance of being a Rescuer

30-50 High chance of being a Rescuer

THE DESPERATE

"I just need to be loved. It doesn't matter who."

The Desperate is a right-swiping ninja. They lack a specific kind of self-awareness, and their main goal is to fulfill their immediate need for comfort with anyone they meet. The Desperate usually looks for low-risk relationships, dislikes being alone, feels comfortable having multiple one-night stands in a single night, or wants a relationship at any cost.

The Desperate is also adept at acting like a temporary chameleon. If your hobby is skiing at the top of Mount Everest, guess what? Despite never having seen snow, the Desperate will tell you they enjoy skiing there. The Desperate focuses on figuring out precisely what you like and quickly adapting those behaviors to get what they want by any means necessary.

The key trait of the Desperate is their willingness to try new things. While this sense of adventure shows an openness to experience, the Desperate often don't realize that people fall in love with the traits they display at the start of a relationship. If those traits aren't maintained, the Desperate risk burning out from the demands of the partner who fell in love with qualities the Desperate no longer show.

A man named Jason once told me that his goal was to sleep with as many women as possible before he reached the age he felt was right to settle down. In his pursuit of numerous sexual partners, he became caught in an addictive routine of swiping right on multiple women's profiles on Tinder. For him, it was all about numbers. Swiping right on one hundred women gave him a 30% chance of matching, a 20% chance of getting a response, a 15% chance of securing a date, and a

10% chance of a hookup. Many times, Jason found himself confusing one woman for another. He became skilled at adopting different personas in his quest for a hookup, often pretending to be whatever his potential partner needed to achieve his goal. Eventually, he forgot who he truly was and what he enjoyed, which led him to waste time when he finally settled down, as he never asked himself the key questions this book would later teach him.

- What kind of person do I desire?
- Where can I locate that person?
- Will our personalities and aspirations align?

The Desperate is also highly sensitive to rejection and will do whatever it takes to avoid it. Jason often found himself willing to deny his happiness to maintain his pursuit of a subsequent relationship.

In the clinical field, the Desperate may have a core personality disorder called borderline personality disorder—a disorder characterized by a primary symptom of fear of abandonment, constant feelings of emptiness, and exaggerated efforts to avoid being left. Erickson's stages of development suggest that the Desperate may be stuck in the trust versus mistrust stage, where individuals learn to bond and trust a potential caregiver.

The Desperate's identity also relies heavily on their potential partner, meaning they see you as an extension of themselves. For example, if you are attractive, successful, and great in bed, the Desperate view themselves as those things too and will try to adapt to match. If rejection happens, the Desperate feel a sharp blow, implying they are not those things, and will increase their efforts to keep you or their next partner.

While a person's desperate status exists on a spectrum, the mildly and highly desperate represent two different people. You can feel mildly desperate after years without a relationship, and that's perfectly normal. You can also be highly desperate and willing to sacrifice your integrity, sanity, and finances to find any person.

A core thing to watch out for is the spectrum. For instance, a Highly Desperate person is susceptible to trauma. "He or she has only hit me once...maybe twice...okay, it happens more often than it should...but he or she still loves me." The Desperate may feel stuck in a relationship and go to counterproductive lengths to regain their partner's affection. For example, they might cheat, flirt, throw a tantrum, fake an illness, or always have some family issue to keep you engaged and interested.

The Desperate and the Rescuer can simultaneously be the best and worst combination. Both feed off each other like peanut butter and jelly, but not for long.

Norma, a middle-aged woman who had been single for ten years after leaving an abusive relationship, believed she was in a better mental space to open her heart to someone again. Her children were older and independent. Her heart had healed, and she could see the joy of life again. She had advanced her career, improved her living conditions for her three children, and created a healthier environment than their father's. Despite all this, Norma felt a sense of emptiness because she longed for a man in the household who could be the ideal husband and father figure. Enter Charlie, her eldest son's basketball coach. He might not seem like much at first glance, but he was good with her children. Norma soon found herself fantasizing about what life would be like with him.

Conversely, Charlie saw Norma as an overwhelmed single mother and tried to keep the children involved in sports by connecting them with other coaches he knew. The truth is, Charlie was a great coach. Husband? Not so much. In less than three months, Norma managed to start a conversation with Charlie that included the children, went on a date, and eventually began a romantic relationship. Because Norma is a single mother of three with limited time, the only way she could see Charlie was by inviting him into her home, around the children. At first, it was perfect. Soon, Norma began to notice traits she didn't like. Charlie never held a full-time job, was not tidy, and struggled with the children outside of sports. But Norma held on because she had fallen into the trap of the Sunk Cost Fallacy. This phenomenon causes people to stay in unhealthy situations because of their prior investments. Soon, it became more convenient for Norma to move Charlie in, and he became her fourth child. Norma did whatever it took to maintain the relationship: she worked extra hours, spent more time away from the children, lied to her friends and family to keep up appearances, and even sacrificed her only vehicle for him. Norma convinced herself she was doing all this to avoid disappointing her children, which would ultimately lead to losing their respect.

The Desperate are stuck in a cycle of disappointment. Here it goes: I failed; I must not fail again. I must win and win all the time. If I fail, then I'm a failure. If I win, then I'm a winner. The Desperate are trapped in a fear-of-failure cycle, creating more setbacks in hopes of winning an already lost race. Sometimes, it's easier to let go. The questions in this will guide you on how to unravel from being Desperate.

DESPERATE PERSONALITY TEST

Questions below are rated on a scale from 1 to 5, with 5 indicating strong agreement and 1 indicating strong disagreement. A score of 3 is considered neutral. Add up your scores for each dating personality type. The answer with the highest score is most likely your dating personality type.

1. *I want attention from anyone who can give me a chance.*
2. *I want to love someone regardless of whether they can love me back.*
3. *I dislike being single.*

4. Even when justified, I see breakups as a chance to bring my lover closer, no matter what, and I will keep trying.
5. I'm willing to do things I dislike to keep my potential partner from leaving.
6. I bounce from one relationship to another with people I know aren't right for me.
7. I often find myself drawn to relationships with people who are not my ideal match.
8. Sometimes, I'm unsure about my type, so I go with whoever approaches me.
9. I often remain in unhealthy situations because I fear being alone.
10. Even when there are several red flags, I tend to tell myself that I can make it work no matter what happens.

TOTAL SCORE: _____

0-15 Low chance

15-30 Medium chance

30-50 High chance

VICTIM

"Everybody in my life has done me wrong."

If you've ever spent a first date listening to your potential partner talk about how horrible their ex is, run! Why? In simple terms, the victim has not yet realized that it takes two to tango. No matter how "bad" your previous partner was, there are elements of fault that one needs to take personal responsibility for to transform from a victim to a survivor. Until an individual does this, there is no healing.

The Victim has a series of failed friendships, romantic, and familial relationships. They perceive the world as a danger zone filled with people who have hurt them and often discuss this pain in excessive detail.

Jennifer, a fifty-year-old divorced woman, has faced the worst luck since birth. Her father was an abusive alcoholic who spent more time cheating on her mother than being a parent or husband. Jennifer vowed never to let that happen to her and ridiculed her mother for tolerating her father's behavior.

In her first year of high school, Jennifer started dating a senior who acted as a protector. He recognized Jennifer's pain and promised to keep her safe from it. Sometimes, she would call him to vent about her father's behavior. Over time, Jennifer noticed strange behaviors in her boyfriend and blamed him for cheating without reason. Eventually, this caused frustration for him, leading him to make abusive comments in self-defense. "You're insecure!" "You need help!" "Stop acting crazy!"

Jennifer, realizing this, began to complain to her friends about him, but she always went back to him because she knew she was sometimes wrong. Knowing this, he gradually started to push boundaries, and she never left. By the time he went to college, he had cheated on her ten times. Yet, she stayed. During her senior year of high school, she decided she didn't need to use protection during sex because she was convinced he would be with her forever. Jennifer had a baby shortly after, and he disappeared. This bitterness grew, and another man she often confided in took on the roles of both father and partner. He left in less than two years because the bitterness seeped into their relationship.

Jennifer's story highlights four core principles.

The Victim's behaviors are very draining: People don't like hearing complaints and bitterness repeatedly. The Victim's emotional state leads to a constant need to rescue, as the Victim is comfortable in pain and stuck in the problem instead of finding a solution.

The Victim is vulnerable to abuse: I used to think it was ironic that focusing on abuse only leads to more abuse. However, after ten years in my career, I realized that dwelling on abuse should be temporary, and the primary focus should be on healing, forgiving, and letting go. If you see yourself as a victim, you'll create a self-fulfilling prophecy that the world is against you.

The Victim is unhealed: hurt people, hurt people. Unknown to the Victim, there is power in healing and forgiving. Remaining in the hurt will eventually hurt your partner and bring out the worst in them. See yourself as a survivor, and the universe will begin to respond accordingly.

The Victim will make you a villain: It's tough to change how people perceive the world. You can apply kindness, but that kindness tends to be short-lived, and failing to meet the Victim's expectations will turn you into a villain.

Jennifer eventually got married and continued to blame everyone but herself. Her husband was a saint. He endured it for years, but gradually started to feel disconnected as she constantly compared him to her exes, who had hurt her in the past. Jennifer created a self-fulfilling prophecy and became her mother. In counseling, I focused the sessions on taking responsibility for ignoring red flags, failing to set boundaries, showing passive behaviors, and fearing abandonment. Jennifer made significant progress in healing and soon found herself shifting from the victim mindset to the survivor mindset.

VICTIM PERSONALITY TEST

Questions below are rated on a scale from 1 to 5, with 5 indicating strong agreement and 1 indicating strong disagreement. A score of 3 is considered neutral. Add up your scores for each dating personality type. The answer with the highest score is most likely your dating personality type.

1. *I don't understand why I keep getting hurt by everyone who says they love me.*
2. *I cannot get over the pain from years ago.*
3. *I am still very resentful towards all my exes.*
4. *I already know I am going to be hurt. It is something I expect at this point.*
5. *Everybody has red flags; there's no point trying to avoid them.*
6. *All men/women are evil.*
7. *I was perfect in all my relationships; they still hurt me.*
8. *I consciously or unconsciously get people to feel sorry for me.*
9. *I tend to focus more on what's going wrong than what's going well.*
10. *I have no control over my relationships.*

TOTAL SCORE: _____

0-15 Low chance

15-30 Medium chance

30-50 High chance

THE SCULPTOR

"I can make you what I want."

The Sculptor is a visionary with an unrealistic direction. Simply put, the Sculptor's goal is to make you desire what they desire, rather than focusing on who you are or what you want. One of the key characteristics of the Sculptor is being a dreamer. The Sculptor has always known what their ideal wife or husband should look, possess, or do.

In some cases, the Sculptor is literally what the name suggests. For instance, it is not uncommon for celebrity men to sculpt their partners through suggested plastic surgeries. A boob job, tummy tuck, or Brazilian butt lift can be done on any woman. Why bother finding a woman who already fits that description?

The Sculptor is lazy. Rather than finding someone who meets their ideal, they try to make the person they're with fit their ideal. Looks aren't the only thing the Sculptor is preoccupied with; they are also concerned with behavioral images. For instance, it is not uncommon for women to find ways to make their potential mate the ideal mate; for example, they may need to give me this, show me that, treat me in a certain way, walk in a certain way, talk in a certain way, etc.

There's nothing wrong with trying to improve your partner's characteristics. Suggesting your partner work out, adopt healthier diet strategies, learn how to treat you, or act differently in front of others is normal until it becomes an obsessive preoccupation.

Jane, a woman in her twenties, met Johnny while attending medical school. Unlike Jane, Johnny was a rough, blue-collar worker who didn't own a suit. Jane, preoccupied with class, fine dining, luxury, and exotic living, found Johnny's outfit of dirty jeans and a white t-shirt disturbing. Jane spent her weekends shopping for Johnny and revamping his entire wardrobe. However, Jane soon became upset about Johnny's choice to use his hands to eat in specific settings. She attempted to teach him some etiquette, but that led to backlash. Johnny would say, "C'mon, you met me at a rundown bar, and we sparked things up; why are you trying to change me?" Jane would respond, "It's just a suggestion." Johnny ignored this red flag, and before long, he was getting haircuts every week to stay groomed, switching to more fashionable outfits after his construction job, and becoming preoccupied with not embarrassing Jane in front of her medical school friends.

To Jane, Johnny was improving. To Johnny, he was losing himself. Jane dropped subtle comments about how she likes to be treated as a woman and how she likes to be treated as his future wife, and slowly, Johnny realized that that wasn't him. He didn't want a mansion in Beverly Hills. He was content with a three-bedroom home that had the basics of life. As a construction worker, he made more than enough money to afford the luxuries of life, but didn't care about Louis Vuitton bags or Gucci clothes. He was a simple man who was okay with two pairs of Jeans and ten wrinkled shirts and t-shirts.

For their wedding, Johnny was comfortable having something in his hometown. Meanwhile, Jane wanted something that would cost $100,000.

The Sculptor is concerned about their image and sees you as a reflection of them. If you look good, they look good. If you look bad, they look bad. However, consult someone who has had plastic surgery. If care is not taken, you will notice multiple flaws that require correction. The Sculptor fails to realize that you can't permanently change someone, and the decision to change should be left to the individual.

In 2020, I met a classic Sculptor with a classic Desperate. The two were a match made in heaven. The Sculptor, Jake, made more than enough money to make more than enough money. His partner, Shelby, allowed Jake to do whatever he wanted. When their relationship was in chaos, neither could identify what caused the demise. Shelby instantly began "liking" sports despite not watching a single event in her earlier life. Interestingly, Jake did not have to say much to Shelby. He just had to suggest subliminal hints. "I used to have a thing for blonde women—very hot." Shelby, a redhead, visited her hairstylist and completely transformed her look. Of course, Jake loved it, and his increased libido made Shelby stick to the blonde hair for two years. Soon, Jake's subliminal hints became less subliminal and more direct and costly. Shelby had five plastic surgeries and could barely be recognized from her previous picture. Like every Sculptor, Jake began to run out of suggestions and soon became bored. Shelby then began to ramp up her looks based on what type of women Jake stared at the most. Shelby and Jake began feeding off each other until an explosion happened in their relationship.

In my session, Jake said, "I give her everything she wants. Heck! She has my credit card and no limit. What else does she want?" I asked him to look at her and ask her the question he asked me, and her response was, "I'm tired of trying to be the idea of who you want me to be, and I just finally want to be me."

The Desperate and the Sculptor have hope because, at some point, reality kicks in, and there's the realization that whatever you're looking for is already out there. Jake, the Sculptor, discovered that he could obtain precisely what he desired with his money, which led to infidelity. Shelby gave up and allowed her natural red hair to return. What he saw as defiance was Shelby beginning to return to a space of self-love. The two broke up. Cycles can only end with awareness.

SCULPTOR PERSONALITY TEST

Questions below are rated on a scale from 1 to 5, with 5 indicating strong agreement and 1 indicating strong disagreement. A score of 3 is considered neutral. Add up your scores for each dating personality type. The answer with the highest score is most likely your dating personality type.

1. *Creating what I want is easier than finding it.*
2. *I often notice issues with my partners that need fixing.*
3. *I find it challenging to distinguish between suggestions and impositions.*
4. *My past partners have accused me of trying to change them.*
5. *I view my partner as a personal project to shape into someone ideal for me.*
6. *My partner reflects me; therefore, they must meet my standards.*
7. *I take pride in the work I have accomplished with my partner.*
8. *I cringe inside whenever my partner says they want to be themselves.*
9. *There is always room for improvement until it is perfect.*
10. *Red flags allow me to mold my partner into what I think is a green flag.*

TOTAL SCORE: _____

0-15 Low chance

15-30 Medium chance

30-50 High chance

THE ROYAL

"Life is about me. Spoil me. Pamper me. Cater to my needs, and I'll keep you in my life."

Treating your partner like a King or Queen is fine. There's nothing wrong with that. You can open doors, pay their bills, and focus your entire life on them, and life can be great. However, the Royal is different. The Royal is a typical King or Queen who has subjects. The Royal doesn't return your treatment because they unconsciously see you as their subject. The Royal cares less about what you need and instead focuses their entire relationship on how you treat them.

Everyone who has a Royal as an ex believes their ex has narcissistic traits. That's not true. Since the Age of Enlightenment, the Royals have often been labeled narcissists. However, for clarity, I want to clarify that a person can exhibit narcissistic traits without having a diagnosis of narcissistic personality disorder.

The Royal can do no wrong. The Royal finds no reason to apologize because they are unaware that they can be wrong. It is not because they are actively trying to hurt you. Nothing clicks. If you have watched any TV show with Kings and Queens, you'll notice that they don't apologize or take accountability. The Royals don't act like victims and rarely speak negatively about their exes, except when they fail to meet their standards. The Royals are not interested in being Sculptors because...that's too much work. You must already have enough money or know how to treat a Royal, or you will meet endless frustrations.

You'll always find the Royal actively seeking pampering from others. Royals have multiple subjects who can provide the "pampering" if one partner isn't enough. A Royal delivers judgment with precision. "I only date men who make six-figure salaries." "If she can't cook me a meal, make me a sandwich, and leave me alone with my beer at nighttime, I don't want it." "I can't wear an engagement ring that does not have a diamond the size of a bowling ball on my fingers." "Vacation within the States? Ew! Let's leave the country, first class, five-star hotel, etc."

The truth is, there is nothing wrong with standards. However, the Royal goes too far by not offering reciprocity to their partners. The Royal either gives nothing or the bare minimum.

I once had a client who joked about spending her husband's paycheck each month while only buying him underwear for his birthday. She believed it was her God-given right for her husband to spoil her excessively. He worked so much and was lucky to get dinner if she was in a good mood... but she would call him at 6:30 p.m. when he was on his way home to buy sushi.

The Royal is spoiled. My encounters with Royals have shown that they were either spoiled in childhood or were exposed to a partner who pampered them during their early dating years. A woman on social media went viral for attempting to embarrass a man for taking her to a Cheesecake Factory. Although they barely knew each other, she felt entitled to be taken to a more expensive restaurant because of the effort she put into her appearance. She shared his face on social media and posted the video. Unfortunately, the opposite effect occurred.

The Royal understands that if "I put more effort into myself, people will worship me." Since the royal needs to be worshipped, they must create a space worthy of that worship. To achieve this, the Royal spends time becoming worthy of worship. For male Royals, toxic masculinity often intensifies, and the pressure to accumulate excessive wealth also increases. Male Royals wield money as power, while female Royals use their beauty for control.

If you're dating someone and the entire basis of the first three dates involves you making sacrifices to impress while receiving only the bare minimum in return, run! Royals will watch you sacrifice all ten fingers when they already have twenty. The Royal is comfortable watching you drown as long as they are safely floating.

ROYAL PERSONALITY TEST

Questions below are rated on a scale from 1 to 5, with 5 indicating strong agreement and 1 indicating strong disagreement. A score of 3 is considered neutral. Add up your scores for each dating personality type. The answer with the highest score is most likely your dating personality type.

1. *My partner's role is to spoil and pamper me.*
2. *I put minimal effort into my relationships because I expect my partner to contribute more.*
3. *I'm working on improving myself to earn the right to be spoiled.*
4. *I avoid arguments or conversations that make me appear to be the bad guy.*
5. *Most of my exes would say I struggle to take accountability.*
6. *My partner reflects who I am; therefore, they must meet my standards.*
7. *I see no reason to accept less when I have several options.*
8. *I feel bored when the focus isn't entirely on pleasing me.*
9. *If I meet someone who can offer me more, I quickly jump ship.*
10. *I prefer things on my terms.*

TOTAL SCORE: _____

0-15 Low chance

15-30 Medium chance

30-50 High chance

THE CHILD

"Why do I need to grow up when I already have everything I need?"

Among all the Daters, the Child is by far the most frustrating person to date. The Child cannot take the initiative to grow up. Typically, the Child is stuck in a particular stage of development and cannot progress from that. Erik Erikson's stages of development suggest that the child is stuck in the "industry versus inferiority stage," which is the stage that requires productivity and competency.

The Child may have a job but still be unproductive. The Child can be a forty-something-year-old man or woman who is stuck in a teenage job, acts immaturely, cannot make decisions on their own, doesn't know how to be an adult, and is being coddled by an older caregiver who is excessively tolerant of the Child's inability to grow up.

The Child is usually carefree and lives for today because there's no point in saving money when there's someone to depend on. The Child has been enabled to such an extent that it's hard to undo, even by a partner. The Child tends to stay in this role if someone continues to enable these behaviors.

The Child is content with life as it is until something drastic happens. The Child has no reason to change because a past partner or parent didn't require them to or didn't speak the language that compelled them to. In some rare cases, the Child may have a well-paying job but is irresponsible about life.

The child is highly dependent. During the first three dates, consider going to the child's apartment. You'll gain insight into other areas of their lives where you may need to take on a parental role. For instance, Jamie had a great job as a banker. However, he spent his free time playing video games, ordering pizza, and maintaining a messy apartment. He met Chloe on Tinder, and the two hit it off during their first three dates. Due to unknown circumstances, Chloe could not visit Jamie's home until after the sixth date. When she visited for the first time, she was horrified by what she saw—a situation she still contends with today. Jamie had no laundry hamper, so his clothes were scattered across the floor. The clean and dirty clothes were mixed, resulting in what Jamie called a game of Russian Roulette with his wardrobe. There was trash everywhere, and the lack of kitchen utensils indicated that Jamie had never used the stove. Although Jamie cleaned his apartment to impress his partner, it was still evident that he was a child when it came to his furniture priorities. For example, even though Jamie earned $7,000 a month, he had no sheets on his bed. His furniture consisted of mismatched colors and bore several permanent food stains. Jamie's gaming area appeared to be the most expensive part of his apartment, and it was instantly clear to Chloe that she would have to assume a maternal role.

The child may force you to compete with the parent: Steve Harvey's best-selling book, "Act like a lady, think like a man," touches on this topic. Because the child may still depend on a parental figure, you may compete with that in your future partner's life. This commonly occurs with momma's boys or daddy's girls. This type of competition creates a natural friction between you and your future partner's parental figure. Chris, a glorified mama's boy, had a stable job but lived with his mother. His mother, who had been single for over ten years, dedicated her life to her only son. Stephanie met Chris at a work convention, and they quickly went on several dates. Stephanie started acting as a girlfriend, but was frequently interrupted by Christopher's mother, who constantly involved herself in their relationship. Christopher's mother would correct Stephanie on how to cook perfect fried chicken for her son, get upset when Christopher chose Stephanie over her, and sometimes show up unexpectedly at Stephanie's apartment to make sure her son was "safe."

On multiple occasions, Stephanie begged Chris to set boundaries with his mother, but Chris always responded, "I'm all she has; I need you to be understanding." Stephanie tried to understand but noticed that Chris would always put his mother first, even after they married. Because Stephanie loved Chris, she gave in and allowed his mother to move in with them. To this day, jealousy exists between Stephanie and her mother-in-law, and now Stephanie is dealing with her mother-in-law telling her how to parent their young child.

The child typically struggles with managing finances. This is one of the most challenging aspects to address with the child, as financial stability is a significant predictor of divorce and future breakups. The child spends money as if it will always be available and has little understanding of the future. This behavior is often a result of the child living under the influence of an enabling caregiver, usually a parent. There is a bias regarding the child. Depending on the context, female children experience less stigma than male children.

A good example is Sasha. Sasha grew up in a two-parent household and was the youngest of seven children. Because she was the only daughter, her father and brothers spoiled her excessively. Unlike her brothers, Sasha never had to find a summer job; she always had the latest toys and clothes, and she never understood what "no" meant. When she was sixteen, Sasha's father died of a severe heart attack. Sasha experienced a profound grief, and her brothers stepped in to make sure she did not feel the full impact of her father's death. She became overly dependent on her family and struggled to keep a job for more than three months. As the youngest, no one gave it much thought until she started dating. Her first serious boyfriend was a much older man who met all her financial needs. They dated for two years; he spoiled her with luxurious vacations and gifts. Everything was fine until they moved in together. Lucas started to notice she rarely cleaned, couldn't cook, and struggled to hold a job. He overlooked these issues because he had enough money to cover her weaknesses, but he realized she relied on him for everything. He excused her behavior until her mother passed away, and he recognized he was stuck with a wife who lacked basic life skills and couldn't care for their daughter like an adult. Frustrated, he sought counseling. In therapy, I had to tell Lucas that he was part of the problem by enabling Sasha. You cannot expect a child to learn to walk if you keep protecting them from falling.

Last but not Least, the Child throws tantrums like any typical kid because of emotional immaturity, as emotional regulation was not taught during childhood.

There are elements of the Child that can change over time. However, it is essential to remember that, like a real child, patience, consistency, and positive reinforcement are required.

THE CHILD PERSONALITY TEST

Questions below are rated on a scale from 1 to 5, with 5 indicating strong agreement and 1 indicating strong disagreement. A score of 3 is considered neutral. Add up your scores for each dating personality type. The answer with the highest score is most likely your dating personality type.

1. *Financially, I live for today.*
2. *I am overly attached and dependent on one of my parents.*
3. *I have always depended too heavily on my partner for basic life skills.*
4. *My friends say I have a dependent personality.*
5. *I'm unable to stand up to my parents because I'm dependent on them.*
6. *My parents still maintain a significant influence over my life and relationships.*

7. *I often choose people who are more mature or adult-like than I am to compensate for my shortcomings.*

8. *It's not that I don't want to grow up; it's that I don't see why I should when life can be easy.*

9. *I feel like I have childlike temper tantrums when things don't go my way.*

10. *Adulting is not my thing.*

TOTAL SCORE: _____

0-15 Low chance

15-30 Medium chance

30-50 High chance

THE INNOCENT

"I don't know what I'm doing."

The Innocent has little to no experience with dating. The Innocent is sweet, kind, and loves love. The Innocent has no defenses and is experiencing many things for the first time. Most people have their first date in high school, but some religious groups discourage dating until much later.

The Innocent's sexual experience might be limited to a kiss or oral sex, which could lead to feelings of guilt or confusion. The Innocent is sensitive. In the dating world, the Innocent faces a high risk of getting hurt. At first, you may feel drawn to the Innocent because of "Awe," but remember that being in a relationship with the Innocent also comes with a lot of responsibility.

What you do while dating an Innocent sets the tone for how they see life. Sometimes, the Innocent will meet another Innocent, and things will go well. Other times, the Innocent may meet a Desperate, Royal, Sculptor, or Child, and is sure to get hurt. Here are some things to know when dating an Innocent.

If you won't be serious, don't bother hurting an Innocent. It comes with a lot of guilt later in life. The Innocent is privy to naivety and may be taken advantage of physically, financially, or sexually.

Dating an Innocent doesn't mean the Innocent will stay Innocent. In my experience working with Innocents, I've seen a stronger curiosity about what else is out there when their current relationship offers no satisfaction. This makes the Innocent aware of the possibility of serial monogamy. Claire, an Amish Innocent who escaped her culture, had never been with anyone. She never learned how to express her sexuality. Soon, Claire met a man who understood some of her trauma, took her in, and acted as her Rescuer. Their relationship was successful, providing a level of security unmatched. However, after five years with her Rescuer husband, she encountered a classic bad boy who promised her nothing but a thrill that would change her life. Over the years, Claire's innocent fantasies grew, and she began daydreaming about Jakobi, who made her feel desired and sexualized. One day, after work, she gave in. Her limited experience in the dating world had kept her from noticing red flags, and Jakobi quickly became possessive and controlling, demanding she leave her husband. She cried daily but continued to be blackmailed with more sexual encounters. One unfortunate day, Jakobi contacted her husband after being ignored for days. It ended their marriage, leaving Claire with no one.

Most people need to experience different things before marriage to help determine the type of person they want to settle down with. Without this, confusion often arises after entering a committed relationship. When I counsel individuals experiencing relationship stress, I gather details about the personalities of all their ex-partners, the events that occurred, and the lessons learned from those relationships. Each time, I notice a pattern, and I tell people that the universe will keep sending the same types of individuals until they figure out exactly who they want to be with.

Claire learned that she broke the heart of a genuinely good man and paid the price through several failed dates before she found her way back to him.

Due to their lack of experience, the Innocent may have unrealistic expectations about Love. This is one of the most frustrating aspects of dating an Innocent Person. They may hold a Cinderella fantasy and expect everything always to be perfect. Be patient. Over time, the Innocent will realize that relationships are like rollercoasters and that "all or nothing" thinking isn't enough.

The Innocent can remain attached to you for a lifetime. Since you are the first person an Innocent dates, their feelings for you are often open and limitless. This difficult-to-break bond can lead to an unhealthy attachment. How you treat the Innocent will also influence how deeply they become attached to you.

The Innocent flourishes best with another Innocent who is content. In the age of social media, we are constantly exposed to temptation. Temptation is safe if there's certainty about who you want to be with. Without that certainty, issues arise. Two Innocents who meet each other's criteria and have an 80% match based on the questions in this book will be perfect together and last forever. I have known many high school sweethearts who never looked back after meeting each other and have never been with anyone else. Both individuals learned to satisfy their emotional, sexual, and physical needs through multiple failed attempts. I once counseled a couple who had been together for over thirty years on how they remained faithful, and the husband joked, "I'm satisfied with my wife because she has multiple personalities. Being with her is like being with different women at once."

If you encounter an Innocent Person, please ensure your intent is pure.

THE INNOCENT PERSONALITY TEST

The questions below are rated on a scale from 1 to 5, where 5 indicates strong agreement and 1 indicates strong disagreement. A score of 3 is considered neutral. Add up your scores for each dating personality type. The answer with the highest score is most likely your dating personality type.

1. I have limited experience in relationships.

2. I enter relationships to love deeply and without reservation.

3. I have little to no sexual experience.

4. I fall in love too quickly.

5. I want my love life to resemble the romance novels I read.

6. I tend to believe what people say without questioning.

7. Love is worth the potential pain.

8. I fantasize about a happily ever after.

9. I have never felt heartbreak.

10. I feel fragile when approaching relationships.

TOTAL SCORE: _____

0-15 Low chance

15-30 Medium chance

30-50 High chance

THE CHAMELEON

"I don't know who I am. I'll be who you want me to be."

Though the Chameleon and the Desperate sound similar, one main difference is that the Chameleon isn't desperate. The Chameleon doesn't have a fixed personality. Its personality, behavior, and character change with each relationship, and they tend to be okay with those changes. Chameleons also tend to quickly mold and adapt to their partner and their partner's family.

It may seem odd, but it's likely a survival tactic learned in childhood. I noticed that most Chameleons were exposed to multiple caregivers growing up. For example, a client who was once an Innocent eventually became a Chameleon because of her experiences in various foster homes. Due to moving between these homes, she lacked a stable environment to develop a strong sense of self. She learned to adapt to each situation to survive.

Being a Chameleon is a trauma response and a form of people-pleasing that can change with trauma counseling. If you are dating a Chameleon, you will notice that things happen way too fast because the Chameleon is comfortable with speed. The good thing is that Chameleons tend to be faithful because it is less stressful to sabotage each relationship.

Cassandra grew up in multiple foster homes. At seventeen years old, she had her first boyfriend, who happened to be her foster parents' biological child. Cassandra's foster mother noticed that Cassandra was suddenly overly obedient, which was highly unusual in her fifteen years as a foster parent. Cassandra began taking on her son's hobbies and became a more integral part of the family than her biological siblings. One day, her foster mother caught her having sex with her biological son. Child Protective Services was informed, and to follow protocol, she had to leave the first love of her life.

Cassandra did not shed a tear. She bottled her emotions in and geared up for the next foster home. Every six months, she was in a different relationship, with a new set of outfits, a different taste in music, and new hobbies. Cassandra was twenty-nine when she finally asked, "Who am I?" It took her three more years to form a concrete identity to attract the right person.

Remember, the distinction between a Chameleon and a Desperate is "choice". Desperates are intentional about changing or deceiving. Chameleons naturally change as a means to survive or feel accepted.

THE CHAMELEON PERSONALITY TEST

Questions below are rated on a scale from 1 to 5, with 5 indicating strong agreement and 1 indicating strong disagreement. A score of 3 is considered neutral. Add up your scores for each dating personality type. The answer with the highest score is most likely your dating personality type.

1. *I become who my partner wants me to be.*
2. *I sometimes feel uncertain about my identity outside of my current relationship.*
3. *I want to be who my partner desires.*
4. *I fall in love too quickly.*
5. *I have a different personality in friendships and relationships.*
6. *I don't just want to be accepted by my partner; I also adjust my personality to accommodate different family members.*

TOTAL SCORE: _____

0-10 Low chance

11-20 Medium chance

21-30 High chance

THE GEM COLLECTOR

"I do not need to commit. My goal is to conquer."

I once met a client who compared dating to Thanos's quest to collect the Infinity Stones. When I initially considered this dating personality type, I wanted to name it "the non-committer," but I realized that these individuals should not have "commitment" in their vocabulary. Gem Collectors thrive on creating chaos and are typically free-spirited individuals who may or may not have been hurt in the past.

Chad, a six-foot blonde Caucasian male with blue eyes, was destined to be a Gem Collector from birth. Elementary and middle school girls flocked to him like bees to a hive. Chad never had to try, and since he never had to try, he decided in 8th grade to sleep with over a hundred women before finally settling down.

Chad developed a plan to stay fit, increase his alcohol tolerance, and attend as many parties as possible. To remain desirable and popular, he engaged in activities that would enhance his reputation: sports, high academic honors, and an aggressive pursuit of success. Chad often referred to dating as "hunting" and maintained a roster of women he could call on his phone. To minimize hurt and damage to women, Chad ensured that he never slept with any woman more than twice. He discovered that one memorable night of passionate sex was sufficient.

The Gem Collector desires to conquer and will say anything to do so. The Gem Collector treats individuals like the stock market. Chad never wanted to spend money on anyone he was dating unless he had to. He prided himself on being minimalistic and would often only have to buy a woman two to three drinks before taking off her pants.

The Gem Collector may be seen as a person without a soul. There comes a point in the Gem Collector's life when the desire to conquer becomes an addiction. The Gem Collector experiences withdrawal and tolerance that surpass even cocaine use. A Gem Collector I counseled described feeling utter emptiness, except when pursuing a conquest. For example, if someone begins using cocaine, they will never feel the same euphoric effect as their first bump, yet they keep chasing that initial high. The Gem Collector sees their quests as the pursuit of that high, which is why they are attracted to individuals who are difficult to obtain and will disappear once they have that person.

The Gem Collector is a classic ghoster, but may reach out to you later if you did something memorable. It is common for the Gem Collector to reach out to you weeks, months, or even years after ghosting you. But remember, patterns will always repeat themselves, and the Gem Collector will do the same thing once he/she has conquered you. Chad always had a list of women to whom he was willing to go back. Often, these women were in committed relationships, and Chad knew he had nothing to lose because they would do anything to feed the ego of being hurt and ignored. Chad will often pursue them relentlessly and whisper sweet nothings into their ears until they give in to another one-night stand.

The Gem Collector was possibly exposed to sexual trauma in childhood or some other type of trauma. Both men and women may experience hypersexuality and reactive attachment after a significant trauma occurs. Jessica, a female Gem Collector, was molested by her stepfather multiple times until she voluntarily began making conscious attempts to seduce her stepfather and take him from her mother. Jessica's journey toward being a Gem Collector came from severe pain and trauma, which led her to learned about the need to control. Jessica once said, "I would rather be in charge than be controlled or taken advantage of ever again." Jessica learned over time that her body could be used to get whatever she wanted and became a Royal and Gem Collector. Her quest was to not only bed these men but also to make them obsessed with her. It gave her a sense of relief and power when they would call her multiple times after a mild sexual encounter. In the process, Jessica hurt over one hundred men a year. Some she slept with, some she teased until they submitted to her will. Jessica once joked and said, "I think I have crack p****y because men run mad over me and are addicted."

Some Gem Collectors can't help it. According to Freud and Carl Jung, the human mind has many unconscious thought processes. Some Gem Collectors are unaware of their unconscious need to pursue this, and they may change when they meet someone who challenges them to see things differently. This may not seem easy to Gem Collectors at first.

When Chad turned thirty, he met a graceful and beautiful lawyer who was an Assured (final dating personality type). Chad tried all his tricks on her, but she didn't budge. She saw through Chad's inner child and his need to conquer, and she never gave in. Chad found himself breaking all his rules for her. He took her on more than ten dates before he could even get a kiss. Soon, Chad started experiencing withdrawals because he dedicated all his energy to just her. Over time, Chad realized he needed therapy, so he landed in my office, where we unpacked everything. Chad explained that although he was still dating this woman, he was constantly rejected, asking, "Why doesn't she want me?" I had to tell Chad that she wanted him, but not his unhealthy version. Ironically, a single act of unconditional love, self-love, and self-control on her part was all Chad needed to change his ways of collecting gems. Chad began to unpack all the pain he had caused other women because of the pain and rejection he was feeling. This lawyer woman never gave up, and Chad eventually made an anniversary post about her. A time came when Chad started to process not wanting to have sex with her due to fear of losing interest and leaving her. I taught Chad the difference between sex and intimacy, explaining, "It's not just about a fuck; it's about emotional connection." Chad is five years sober from Gem Collecting and has become the Assured (final dating personality type).

Gem Collectors will eventually grow weary of the emptiness of their multiple conquests. Professor Bruce Alexander identified that humans' primary desire is to form authentic connections. Genuine connection arises from experiences that enable a person to feel safe. However, it is not your role to change a Gem Collector, as that may lead to disappointment. Gem Collectors only transform when they are ready. The catalyst for this change could be a person, a miraculous shift in perspective, or a challenging experience that prompts insight.

Jessica's gem-collecting ways changed when she started wanting to have children. Her experiences with multiple men helped her realize that having children in an unstable relationship would create a similar nightmare to what she faced with her stepfather. Thus, she shifted from gem-collecting to searching for the ideal man, who happened to be an Innocent. She remained in control and was faithful to him solely to avoid replicating her trauma.

THE GEM COLLECTOR PERSONALITY TEST

Questions below are rated on a scale from 1 to 5, with 5 indicating strong agreement and 1 indicating strong disagreement. A score of 3 is considered neutral. Add up your scores for each dating personality type. The answer with the highest score is most likely your dating personality type.

1. *I'm not interested in committing to just one person.*
2. *I typically seek out relationships that offer immediate benefits.*
3. *I don't care about my body count.*
4. *I fall in and out of love too quickly.*
5. *After I have sex with someone, I become bored.*
6. *I pursue relationships purely for the excitement.*

7. *I end relationships without giving any explanation.*
8. *I dream of a happy ending, but I feel scared when I get too close to someone.*
9. *I self-sabotage my relationships by creating chaos when I get too close.*
10. *A life devoid of love seems safer.*

TOTAL SCORE: _____

0-15 Low chance

15-30 Medium chance

30-50 High chance

THE OBSESSIVE

"I want you every day, all day, to myself and no one else. Please don't leave me, ever!"

The obsessive most likely experiences neglect in childhood and has a morbid fear of abandonment, which causes an insecurity that runs deep into the bones. The Obsessive Person starts a relationship slowly but becomes attached to an individual quickly. Signs that you are dating an Obsessive will be based on the questions below about the Obsessive's past relationship. If the Obsessive has a legal order of protection, run! Run if the Obsessive Person starts creating a lifelong plan for marriage, kids, or anything else before genuinely getting to know you. The Obsessive has elements of the Desperate except that they are picky about who they want. The Obsessive most likely has a type and an innate need to pursue that type.

Two personality disorders prominently exhibit the issues of the Obsessive type. One is borderline personality disorder, commonly known as BPD. Individuals with BPD experience an intense fear of abandonment from any sign of it, regardless of how minor or unrealistic it may be. These individuals will go to great lengths to ensure that abandonment does not happen. People with BPD also experience dysregulated emotional outbursts due to this fear and tend to think in polarized, black-and-white terms about relationships. For example, they might think, "My partner is the best thing that has ever happened," and then suddenly believe, "My partner is the worst thing that has ever happened." This pattern of devaluation and overvaluation can confuse the partner, and if the partner is a Rescuer, it can create a manic cycle in the relationship.

Another personality disorder that explains the obsessive-compulsive disorder is Histrionic Personality Disorder—a disorder characterized by attention-seeking behaviors. The Obsessive does not care whether the attention is positive or negative, as long as there is attention. The Obsessive may fake illnesses, create chaos, lie, embarrass you, or generate a need always to be rescued to keep you involved. Please don't fall for it.

If you're trying to avoid an Obsessive, remember that even responding to a text message fuels the need for an Obsessive to keep pursuing you. Blocking the obsessive also causes a need that fuels the need: "Oh, I must be important enough to be blocked. Let me try another method."

If you're dating an Obsessive, your instincts will tingle because there's a lack of safety in dating the Obsessive. Obsessive individuals can become violent, lie against you in court, or try to ruin your reputation. The Obsessive is ruled by chaos and should be avoided at all costs. If you can keep your distance, do so.

As a Therapist, I have found that the Obsessive will eventually stop if there is someone else to Obsess about. Here are some things to know about the Obsessive.

Psychological principles govern obsessions and compulsions. Obsessions are persistent thoughts, such as the need to be with a particular person. The compulsion comes with an act, e.g., I'll show up to work with flowers, and if that doesn't work, I'll send gifts to the house. If that doesn't work, I'll make the person my emergency contact at the hospital so they can feel sorry for me for a self-inflicted injury. The Obsessive is stuck in a cycle that can only be broken if the Obsessive realizes that giving power to thoughts causes issues later on. For example, when treating OCD, I remind my clients that every time they wash their hands unnecessarily, they increase the likelihood of having to rewash them. The obsession will always get more substantial if a compulsion follows it.

The key to breaking the obsession is to exaggerate your uselessness regarding their needs. Umar, an Arab American male, once met an Obsessive woman. She was gorgeous, and Umar couldn't understand why she was single at twenty-six. Umar slowly began to realize that she was unstable when she would demand his location, show up randomly at his work, try to isolate him from friends and family, and contact every woman on his social media to stay away from him. Umar felt trapped. The more he tried to push her away, the harder she returned. Umar's family saw her behavior as the ideal wife, as she always showed up to cook, clean, and remind Umar why she needed him. Umar, however, did not tell his friends and family about the outburst she would throw if he decided to leave. She even went as far as trying to commit suicide, and Umar felt so guilty he came back. Every day, Umar felt like the cage was getting tighter. There was no love; there was just pity. He knew she couldn't help it, but didn't know how to leave the situation because she once threatened to claim a false rape if he tried. Umar felt stuck. Since blocking and breaking up, one temporary order of protection and therapy didn't work, Umar gave in.

If the Obsessive loses sight of your "ideal" status, they may lose interest. I urged Umar not to be the ideal mate. Umar began demanding more from her, which created a sense of constant dissatisfaction. Obsessive individuals tend to pride themselves on being "perfect," which is why they are surprised if you feel suffocated by them or want to leave. If that sense of "perfect" is questioned, it leads to several innate issues. It was only a matter of time before she began to lose interest and seek another prey.

Dating an Obsessive can lead to relational trauma. Many of the individuals I have worked with who have dated an Obsessive experienced significant physical, mental, and emotional trauma, which often deters them from dating anyone else again. I often draw an analogy between fireworks and gunshots. Some soldiers returning from traumatic battles in Vietnam reported feeling hypervigilant on the 4th of July because their bodies confused fireworks with gunshots. This same principle applies to relational trauma. Recovering from dating an Obsessive may cause you to push away good people due to that fear. However, if your date respects boundaries during the first three dates, it's a good sign that you're experiencing fireworks rather than gunshots.

THE OBSESSIVE PERSONALITY TEST

Questions below are rated on a scale from 1 to 5, with 5 indicating strong agreement and 1 indicating strong disagreement. A score of 3 is considered neutral. Add up your scores for each dating personality type. The answer with the highest score is most likely your dating personality type.

1. *When I fall in love, I fall very deeply.*
2. *I need to control what my partner wears or does to prevent them from leaving me for someone else.*
3. *I do whatever it takes to stay with my partner when I'm in love.*
4. *Thoughts about what my partner is doing occupy my mind when I'm not with them.*
5. *I want to know what my partner is always doing because I'm afraid they will leave me.*
6. *I would prefer that the world contained only me and my partner so we could have more time for each other.*
7. *My partner doesn't need friends or family when they are with me.*
8. *When my partner becomes distant, I focus on drawing him or her back in.*
9. *I don't accept "no" as an answer and have an intense fear of abandonment.*
10. *I'm willing to look or act out of character if it helps my partner like me back.*

TOTAL SCORE: _____

0-15 Low chance

15-30 Middle chance

30-50 High chance

THE ASSURED

"I know what I bring to the table; I'm not afraid to eat alone."

The Assured has had a significant dating experience and learned from it. They have a healthy dose of self-esteem, self-love, maturity, and respect for others. They know what they want and are not afraid to go after it. The journey towards being assured involves mastering all the questions in this book and being willing to settle for nothing less.

The Assured is unwilling to settle for less than they deserve and is not averse to waiting. This gives the Assured a healthy dose of patience in pursuing their goals. The Assured also doesn't look at a person's words but pays attention to the person's actions as well. If the Assured senses something that doesn't feel right, the Assured is more than willing to leave.

The Assured is not desperate, not innocent, not interested in rescuing or sculpting, doesn't play victim, is not royal, a child, is not a Chameleon, has no interest in collecting gems, and is not obsessive. The Assured knows precisely what they want. If you want to be the Assured, read every question in this book and master it. It won't fail.

The Assured is very likely to meet a healthy partner. They have mastered the art of patience in finding their ideal mate. This patience and willingness to fail give the Assured's energy an attraction towards something tangible and undying. My favorite thing to say in counseling is that hurt people attract hurt people, and healed people attract healed people. If you want a healthy person, you must work towards the healthy behavior you want to see in the other person. A great family therapist and professor I once worked with constantly challenged his clients to write a list of things they want in their partner. After writing the list, he asked his clients to categorize the list into negotiables and non-negotiables. After categorizing the list, he asked his clients to determine a percentage of their ideal partner scores. For instance, at least 80% of the non-negotiables and 35% of the negotiables are included. After completing this task and discussing it thoroughly, he asked his client to write their name at the top and asked them to work towards achieving the goals on the list. Of course, this always blew the minds of his clients, but he would always say If you want your partner to be trustworthy, be trustworthy too. If you want your partner to be fit, go to the gym. If you want your partner to be wealthy, make money too. His idea was that expecting someone to give you something you don't have is a recipe for codependency. He hated statements like "he completes me, or she's my other half." Like him, I believe that everyone needs to be a complete whole before trying to be in a relationship with anyone else.

The Assured is willing to do the work. The Assured knows that love comes with work. The Assured does not have Cinderella syndrome (the belief that life in a relationship will be happily ever after). The Assured keeps their partner accountable and accepts accountability, too. The Assured's unconditional love towards you means you're willing to grow physically, spiritually, emotionally, financially, intellectually, mentally, and socially.

The Assured has a passion of his or her own. This is critical because the Assured knows that life requires balance, and investing everything in your relationship will lead to disappointment. The Assured has a series of goals that must be accomplished outside the relationship. For instance, the Assured invests in themselves to develop their career and has a sense of independence. Remember, the Assured would rather be alone than be in a toxic relationship or with someone unwilling to grow. For this reason, two Assureds getting together is like the ultimate power couple on a mission to slay. My favorite thing to tell couples is, "When two 1s get put together, it is still one". This means that in a relationship, you still need to retain your passion, goals, friendships, relationships with family, lifestyle, and hobbies instead of becoming the Desperate or Obsessive who invests everything into their partner.

THE ASSURED PERSONALITY TEST

Questions below are rated on a scale from 1 to 5, with 5 indicating strong agreement and 1 indicating strong disagreement. A score of 3 is considered neutral. Add up your scores for each dating personality type. The answer with the highest score is most likely your dating personality type.

1. I am confident in my ability to pick the right person for my life because I have worked on myself.
2. I have a firm list of non-negotiables and negotiables in relationships that I abide by.
3. I know my flaws and behaviors that impacted my previous relationship negatively.
4. I would rather be single than be in a toxic relationship.
5. I am confident in what I bring to the relationship.
6. At this point in my life, I know what I want in my career, social, and familial life.
7. I have processed my traumas and understand how they impacted those around me.
8. I am constantly willing to grow and improve.
9. I am only willing to be with someone who is on the same wavelength of growth.
10. A life without love is not love.

TOTAL SCORE: _____

0-15 Low chance

15-30 Middle chance

30-50 High chance

THE DISORGANIZED

The disorganized dating personality type is usually made up of individuals who exhibit all the traits of other dating personalities, depending on the situation or the person they are dating. Potential partners with this personality tend to be uncertain about who they are. If you take the tests listed above and you have multiple high scores, which are relative to your past dating experiences, you're likely disorganized. This isn't necessarily a bad thing if your goal is to become the Assured.

ONE

❦

Question to ask yourself.
How much time do you have?

In a recent counseling session, I met a lady who finally met her dream man. He was everything she wanted and more. He was enlightened about his trauma, aware of all the past mistakes he made in his relationship, said all the right words, confessed his weaknesses, responded appropriately to emotionally charged situations, and understood her love language. She beamed with joy as she described him every session, and the glow never changed for seven months, which I found unusual. Well, she had one problem. She was married. Before you judge her, know that she has been in a loveless relationship for ten years, lives with her husband, stays in separate bedrooms, and has a mutual agreement that their relationship is strictly transactional until the youngest child graduates from high school.

The question I asked her was, "How much time do you have?" She could wait two years for her youngest to graduate, and the man of her dreams could disappear into something more fruitful, or she could make that decision now. Time! Time! Time!

See, none of us knows the future. She could be postponing ultimate happiness for a future that was uncertain. We need to see life as something that can expire at any moment. In a show I used to watch, "A Thousand Ways to Die," I was struck by the dangers that constantly surround us. When I talk about how much time you have, don't just think about death. I want you to think about the opportunity.

When your gut feeling kicks in, it's time to act. A gentleman I worked with spent fifteen sessions talking about a woman he liked at work but couldn't find the courage to approach. In my opinion, she gave him every possible green light. The only thing she could have done to ease his nerves was wear a bold sign saying, "ASK ME OUT!" So, what were the signs? She bought him lunch and invited him several times, initiated a shoulder touch, looked for any reason to visit his office to ask questions, invited him to a house party that he turned down, asked about his life, texted him after hours, and more. Yet, he still didn't make a move. Part of his fear came from the "Me Too" movement. He was terrified of asking her out and spending the next hour in Human Resources to defend a harassment claim. I worked with him session after session, using a powerful cognitive behavioral therapy tool called cognitive reconstruction to help him understand that respectfully saying, "I'd like to take you out on a date someday," wasn't sexual harassment if he recognized that her saying "no" meant "no" and was not an excuse to keep trying. Despite this, he continued to say, "I will ask her out this week." His social anxiety was working overtime, causing him to stumble over his words whenever he got near her. It got to the point where he preferred to enjoy her company as a friend rather than risk making things awkward by asking her out.

Well, time moved on. She got a job in a distant state and gave her two weeks' notice. During this time, he found the courage to ask her out over the phone and confess his love for her, but neither of them could make it work because of the long distance.

Who wasted time in this situation?

The answer is both! She could have slapped him across the head and said, "Ask me out, dumbass." Just kidding, I promise. Or he could have taken a chance at life. Time waits for no one, and it matters a lot. When you meet someone you think you might like, the clock starts ticking on how quickly you can convince them to be part of your life.

At the bar, you have until the last call to make your move. At the mall, you have as much time as it takes for the other person to finish shopping. On a first date, you can give them something meaningful enough to remember you, paving the way for a second date. Life moves quickly, but you can slow down and enjoy it.

The amount of time you have also depends on your age. If you're a teenager navigating the dating scene, you might have plenty of time… maybe. At least if you meet the life expectancy criteria, you do have time. If you're a forty-year-old single father, you might not have as much time due to work, school, and family commitments.

You don't want to waste your time, no matter how much you think you have. This is especially true for women; the biological clock is a real phenomenon. Time moves forward. She got a job in a distant state and gave her two weeks' notice. During this period, he found the courage to ask her out over the phone and confess his love for her, but neither of them could make it work due to the long distance. I know it's a cliché and that there are various methods of childbirth, but scientifically speaking, the risks associated with giving birth increase with age. So, it's time to let go of that guy who has refused to propose after four years! In Beyoncé's famous words, "If you liked it, then you should have put a ring on it." Men, too: while you may not have a ticking biological clock, you do have a financial one. Meeting financial goals and raising a family is best done in your prime. Research shows that both men and women who advance in their careers tend to marry much later in life. Meanwhile, people who prioritize their family often progress in their careers later.

Grow with your family. The mistake I often see is people waiting to be fully established in their careers before venturing on the journey. This is why research shows that people settle down in their late 30s and 40s, compared to their early 20s, just two decades ago. What happens is the dating pool gets so small and narrow; what's left are people who have already been traumatized by past unhealthy relationships, have emotional baggage the size of a Boeing 767, and individuals whose standards are as high as Mount Everest.

Also, when you read this book, you'll understand why those three significant points are priority questions to ask.

Lastly, I will explain why I titled the book Thirty-Three Questions to Ask Before Your Third Date.

Most people wait too long before they ask core questions. What's too long? Anything over four dates! Why? In this "horny culture," sex is more likely to happen after the third date. In some cases, before; in most cases, after. Why? Both individuals may feel comfortable enough to let their private areas touch. Don't get me wrong. I have met individuals who had sex on their first date and stayed together twenty years later, but I have also met more individuals who have had sex on multiple first dates and never met the right person.

Sex is a catalytic confusion designed by nature to confuse our species just enough to procreate. The number of hormones that get released after sex is incredible. Men release outrageous amounts of testosterone, which amplifies their need to have more sex, and women release an outrageous amount of oxytocin, which causes love to flow. This, combined with dopamine, can cause individuals to feel that they are in love rather than in lust. When these individuals realize they are not in love, they are one year in and fearful about counting their losses. So, what happens? The game changes! Let me modify my partner to someone I want so I won't waste time.

With the way holes work, the deeper you dig, the harder it is to get out of the hole. So, what happens? Two more years of traumatic dating get masked with a marriage and kids, and when you feel a little hope, anger ensues.

I need to remind many divorced individuals that the anger isn't directed at their ex-partners; it's directed at themselves for "wasting" time and opportunities to be with someone else.

TWO

------- ⟨⟨◈⟩⟩ -------

Are you married?

What? Are you saying people don't ask? Yep! People don't. There's a common assumption that if someone approaches you without a ring and without a "marriage look," they must be single. That's not true. Even if you meet a nineteen-year-old, it's perfectly okay to ask this question.

Years ago, I was working on a child custody case. As a court-appointed expert witness, I sought to determine which parent was in the child's best interests. During this investigation, I realized the primary source of conflict was Jacob's decision to start a relationship with Jane while going through a divorce. This is a common mistake that occurs more frequently than you might think.

Often, after a couple has declared they want to be separated or divorced, the mistake is the suddenness of returning to the dating pool. Psychologically speaking, this is not because there is a need to have sex with everyone; it's because both individuals have spent years with a companion and are used to having that one person to call at the end of the day or cuddle with. A recently divorced man explained that the emptiness of this was the reason he jumped back into the dating pool. Ironically, this is the reason why second marriages are statistically more likely to end in divorce.

This critical period between separation and the completion of divorce is marked by significant uncertainty. For example, I once met a couple who came to my office for couples counseling less than an hour after they had signed divorce papers at the court. I was confused and asked why now. Both told me that their one-year divorce process made them realize that the grass is not greener on the other side. During my counseling, I inquired about the people they dated while separated and why it didn't work. They offered several reasons, and I realized something: because of their uncertainty, the two individuals had severely hurt the people they dated.

Avoid dating anyone who is married, regardless of the length of the divorce process, because marriage still takes precedence over a new relationship with someone. If someone tells you, "I'm married" and "It's complicated," remind them to simplify their situation before trying to be with you. It is your life, and there's no time to waste. Suppose you are going to obey the other questions in this book; a divorced person needs to have anywhere from six months to a year of healing before thinking about a serious relationship. This healing is essential for creating a healthy relationship.

There is an exception to this rule. Don't date anyone who is married or separated unless you're seeking a casual relationship. Jessica, a busy professional who barely sleeps in her apartment and travels extensively for work, once told me she preferred to date men who were married or separated because she didn't want to commit. It worked well for her, but she judged herself harshly for that choice. It gave her a sense of control since she didn't have to worry about breaking anyone's heart. Now, am I saying you should date a married person if you don't want to be committed? No. I believe in respecting marriage, but if you do choose to do so, make your intentions clear to yourself.

Always ask the question, "Are you married?" because married people who want to cheat have a "don't ask, don't tell policy." Save yourself from future hurt.

THREE

What is your love language?

Gary Chapman made a groundbreaking discovery that many couples therapists still use today—the five love languages. The five love languages include a quiz that helps you identify your love language, which can be found on various online websites. These love languages are acts of service, gift-giving, physical touch, words of affirmation, and quality time.

An act of service is something you do for your potential partner. Some people feel loved when an action makes their lives easier. For example, Jerry said he fell in love with his future wife from the moment he saw her because she remembered the birth dates of his family members and would help him shop for gifts, as he was a "typical man". Jerry said that what he loved most about his wife was that she never forgot his doctor's appointments. Because of this, he always took the initiative to show his love language in return. If your potential partner seems inconsiderate, lazy, and lacks initiative, that's not the partner you want if your love language is acts of service.

For those who believe acts of service mean your partner must serve you, you're mistaken. That's not the essence of acts of service. The act needs to be done with love. For example, if you enjoy cooking for your partner because you love seeing their smiles when they eat your food, you're fortunate! But if you cook for your partner out of obligation, even if you're feeling burnt out, you will start to feel resentment over time. Remember, it must be done with love, not duty.

Physical touch is beyond sex. It includes cuddling, fondling, caressing, stroking, hugging, hand holding, and more. A person whose love language is physical touch will likely want to be close to you often. If you dislike being touched, it's best to avoid someone whose love language is physical touch. Carolynn, a woman in her twenties who endured sexual and physical abuse in the past, preferred sitting on opposite ends of the sofa, disliked handholding and cuddling, and only enjoyed sex if she initiated it and was on top. Ironically, every man she met after leaving her abusive parents' home had "physical touch" as their love language and couldn't understand her hypervigilance around being touched. I recommended EMDR (Eye Movement Desensitization and Reprocessing therapy, mainly used to treat trauma). I also suggested she find a partner with a different love language or one who understands and is sensitive to her trauma. Ask your future partner about their love language, specifically how they prefer to be touched and where they prefer not to be touched. Again, physical touch should be motivated by love, not obligation.

Quality time is something more delicate than people think. In couples counseling, I always tell my clients that there is a difference between quantity and quality time. Many couples have plenty of time, which is driven by survival and day-to-day routines. For example, the average couple wakes up, goes through their morning routine, heads to various workplaces, returns home after errands, sits down for dinner, watches television, sleeps, and repeats. Several text messages and phone calls will be exchanged between these events about the day's progress and possibly dinner plans. There's no pause. Quality time is a lot more intentional. It requires tact, thought, and precision. For instance, a couple once told me that at a specific time every day, they would stop whatever they were doing, pause, and sit together on the phone while eating lunch. They enjoyed the silence of chewing, accompanied by the occasional chit-chat. This twenty- to thirty-minute phone call is an intentional act of quality time. Quality time is centered around two individuals trying to recharge their vibrations to remain one intentionally.

Gift-giving as a love language does not have to be expensive. People get lost in buying bags, Rolexes, cars, and designer clothes for their significant other without pausing to ask, "What meaning does this gift have to our relationship?" For instance, a Rolex is just a Rolex that anyone wealthy enough to afford can give. Now, a Rolex with an engraved message from a loved one becomes not just a gift but also a memory. This kind of gift requires thought, taste, and effort. The receiver of this gift will never forget who gave it to them and how, initially, reading the engraved message made them feel. The power of gift-giving as a love language lies in the effort it takes to obtain, whether financially or physically. If you took the time to customize a jersey for your girlfriend, the effort weighs more than buying one off the shelf.

Words of affirmation are something I believe everyone needs to master. In simple terms, words of affirmation are compliments to your partner, like, "You look beautiful," and "You're just so hot." Words of affirmation can also express gratitude, such as, "I don't know what I would do without you," and "You're just so thoughtful sometimes... I feel lucky to have you." They can also be encouraging and motivating, such as "I know you can do it. You have overcome more challenges than ever," or "You are just so awesome; they would be lucky to have you." The key element of words of affirmation is positive reinforcement that encourages your partner to continue showing love for you. It requires tact and understanding of what your partner needs to hear every time. Words of affirmation aren't simply, "I love you." It is "I love you because..."

It is common for people to have multiple love languages, but most people lean towards one "non-negotiable." There are love languages you like to receive and love languages you find easy to give. If gift-giving comes naturally to you, find someone whose love language is receiving gifts. Life is easier when you and your potential partner share the same love language. Suppose it doesn't; don't fret. Ask yourself how much of the love language your partner gives satisfies you.

Elizabeth, a lesbian woman in her forties, loves hiking, journaling, swimming, and traveling. Her partner's primary love language is physical touch, and she is a diehard introvert who loves being surrounded by four walls. However, Elizabeth, a survivor of childhood sexual abuse, hates excessive body contact. This disconnect made it difficult for both individuals to feel seen and loved. Both gave every love language, but the primary love language was not met, resulting in some dissatisfaction. After mere observation, I realized the relationship was heading towards a breakup because both seemed consumed in themselves. I taught the popular "three circles." You circle, the partner circle, and the overlap between both is "the relationship center." It's okay to hop into each part of the circle. Sometimes, do what works for you. Sometimes, do what works for your partner, and sometimes, do what works for the relationship. You don't have to be stuck in "all-or-nothing thinking."

Your potential partner's love language will appear during the first three dates. Be cautious of Gem Collectors and Desperates when asking this question, as they may pretend to exhibit a specific love language. Just remember, people can only maintain a facade for so long. Give time for true colors to emerge; when you see those colors, trust what you observe. Don't second-guess it.

Here are three simple ways to know if someone naturally has your love language.

a.   They express love to others in their lives through their chosen love language. If someone is a natural "quality timer," you will notice their pursuit of quality time with all their loved ones, not just you.

b.   They remain consistent with their love language, whether or not you give it to them. A person who is a gift giver is a gift giver regardless of whether you reciprocate.

c.   They use love language for themselves as well. A person whose love language is words of affirmation tends to give words of affirmation to themselves, too. Be wary of people who compliment your looks but talk down on their looks—that person has self-esteem issues they may or may not be aware of. Run from individuals who give quality time to everyone but themselves—that person is walking on a short fuse. Cut off individuals who give everyone their time and effort as acts of service, but refuse to ask for help when needed—they are people pleasers. Watch out for people who give without expecting anything in return—they may be controlling. Be careful when you approach someone who is okay with touching but not okay with being touched—they may be traumatized.

FOUR

What is your attachment style?

I Promise I won't waste too much time on this question. Though it is essential, a person's attachment style is difficult to fully grasp due to numerous factors beyond a person's control. However, like your love language, your attachment style matters as much as peanut butter matters to a jelly sandwich. One can go without the other, but it's even better when they're awesomely combined.

A person's attachment style refers to how they form bonds with others. It doesn't have to be a romantic relationship; it could be a friendship or a familial relationship. I emphasize this because you can figure out a person's attachment style during a relationship (Something to keep in mind).

The first is secure attachment. A person with a secure attachment receives nurturing, stability, and consistency, making the person comfortable expressing and receiving emotions from others. The Assured fits typically into this category.

The anxious attachment style is characterized by a deep fear of abandonment due to inconsistent or sudden loss of a significant nurturing relationship. The anxiously attached usually have a negative view of themselves and a positive view of others. The dating personality type that typically falls under this category is the Obsessive because the Obsessive may want to do whatever it takes to avoid abandonment. For obvious reasons, the Desperate will compromise on themselves to find a partnership.

The same inconsistency characterizes the avoidant attachment style, but this time, the avoidantly attached have a favorable view of themselves and a negative view of others. It's simple: they feel better than others and fear being dependent on or depending on others, which leads them to push before others come too close. There is a chronic avoidance of intimacy, which makes the avoidantly attached more likely to be a Gem collector, a Sculptor, or a Royal.

The disorganized attachment style, also known as the fearful-avoidant style, tends to fluctuate between being anxiously attached and avoidantly attached. The disorganized attachment style has a balance of push and pull that describes the Obsessive, the Desperate, and the Rescuer. The Victim is also a dating personality type that falls into this category because of the constant need to gain sympathy from others. It's a fearful push and pull.

You can discover your attachment style by researching different examples online, talking to your therapist, and thoroughly evaluating your life. You can find out your future partner's attachment style by directly asking them the questions in this book, paying attention to the patterns of their past relationships, and simply observing their communication style with you.

FIVE

What was your first relationship like?

I met a couple who had been together for over fifty years. They met in high school and spent their entire relationship with their first love.

It was impressive because both beamed joyfully as they looked at each other. I call these kinds of couples the anomalies. The anomalies are extremely lucky because all six factors that make a positive, long-lasting relationship are met. I haven't discussed the six factors yet, as understanding their importance requires reading the entire book.

First, relationships are fiery and intoxicating. It's like the first time using any drug—the high is always, well… high! It's the first time feeling butterflies in your stomach, an intense energy that draws two people together, a need to want to be around each other, and…you know…the list goes on. Most individuals fail to understand that relationship highs require more work to sustain themselves at this point in their lives. Consistency isn't necessary; there needs to be a variety of flavors. It would be best if you tried different things. Anomalies have mastered this, but since most people won't, understanding a potential partner's first relationship will give you insight into what has or will give them that "high." It's simple. Many couples miss this point because they expect the same energy to be applied or apply less energy, rather than more. People evolve.

Janet's first boyfriend was Christopher, who took pride in being called Christopher, not Chris. Janet fell in love with his confidence, his love for philosophy, his pride in art, and his spontaneity. Every day, there was a variety. They kissed in classrooms, empty fields, in the car, at the mall, everywhere, and at any chance they got. Christopher loved her wildness and spontaneity and rewarded it with gentleness. The two balanced each other and shared multiple great experiences within six months. Distance happened because Janet's military father was stationed hundreds of miles away from each other, and soon, the fights began. It was no surprise when the two ended the relationship abruptly, less than three months later. They never talked, but they have been friends on Facebook.

Okay, fast-forward ten years. Janet is seated in front of a charming young man, and he asks her, "What was your first relationship like?"

She smiles. There's a spark in her eyes. He noticed she started playing with her hair, and then she talked about Christopher in a daze. Now, this gentleman can get three simple points from the description.

1. Janet romanticizes confident men who love philosophy and are somewhat artsy. The gentleman can adopt these traits if he is a Chameleon.
2. Janet never got closure. This means she may not have fully moved on from her ex and is keeping close tabs on him. Closure is critical to move past any relationship. Denying yourself closure from a relationship is dangerous. Whether it is self-induced closure (when a person decides they are utterly done with a relationship and a discussion and understanding are unnecessary) or mutually induced closure (when two people mutually agree to move on after lengthy discussions,

17

understanding, and some maturity), closures can prevent future relationships.

3. Janet is possibly seeking that same high in other men, and if he's not a Chameleon or truly has those traits, there will be an obvious ending.

Christopher had a completely different experience while dating Janet. Because she was wild and spontaneous, he couldn't trust her after she moved. He was stuck on the idea that she was cheating and thought she probably was; there was nothing to control or prevent it from happening. Christopher's future wife approached him with the question, "What was your first relationship like?" He had a bittersweet response, accompanied by a look of uncertainty.

Christopher's future wife asked, "What was your first relationship like?" His response was dark and cold, with a slight hint of wonder mixed in.

1. His response shows that he is still bitter or angry, which suggests that he may require mutually induced closure since he has not reached self-induced closure.
2. This lack of closure may be attributed to a desire to be with Janet again.
3. Understanding Christopher's past relationships will help her determine whether he has overcome them.

❖

What was it like when you first fell in love?

Like the previous question? Na. This is different. A person's first relationship is not necessarily the first time they fell in love. If you hear anyone say, "I didn't know what love was until I met you." It's likely coming from a space of sincerity unless they are confirmed Gem collectors. There are three reasons you should ask this question.

- **To know a person's description of love.** This is a key point in truly understanding how a person wants to love and show love. I once met a woman whose description of her first love was something you would see in a domestic violence educational video. The truth is that love is relative to everyone, and it is essential to explore that. Understanding what a person considers love can give you a glimpse into how they may love you. Patterns rarely change unless awareness is present.

- **To know how recent the individual's love experience was.** Knowing this fact will give you a glimpse into whether someone is over their ex, still harboring resentment towards their ex, or simply aware of why things didn't work out. I have met several individuals in my counseling chair who have tremendous amounts of unresolved feelings about an ex. Yet, their partners were clueless about it. This question gives your future partner insight into their feelings about their former partner. This will also give you a glimpse of how high someone's walls are or their willingness to love again.

- **To know if you have had a similar experience.** Shared experiences typically breed a willingness to improve on that experience later in life.

Tanya, a middle-aged biracial woman, had been through six relationships in her life and claimed to have loved most of them. Tanya was an unfiltered and unbothered woman when it came to love. There was no shame in how she expressed it. However, when it was time to get a commitment from others, they always fell short—except for one Brazilian exchange student who looked just like her when it came to love. He was expressive, desirous, wild, passionate, and unapologetic about his feelings. The two fell deeply in love, and that fire lasted for three years.

One morning, Tanya received a terrible call from a woman claiming to be his wife. Heartbroken, she approached him, and he admitted that he was still married but separated for a divorce. Since then, the two have never stopped fighting because Tanya can't let go of the deep, dark secrets he's kept from her. Eventually, they broke up and never got back together. Tanya considered him her only true love.

Years later, Tanya met a gentleman who was calm, collected, and confident in what he wanted. He was desirous, passionate, friendly, intuitive, and highly intellectual. She was excited to know she could love again. One thing was missing: James wasn't wild or adventurous. His intellectual nature confined him, so his idea of adventure was planning a spontaneous date three weeks ahead. James' instincts knew what Tanya's type was, but he never questioned her decision to be with him.

Years later, Tanya ran into her Brazilian boo, and the fire got so steamy she could not resist his wildness.

When James found out…which didn't take long, he had a flashback when he asked Tanya what her first true love was like. It was no surprise that Tanya had the same look of puppy love just three weeks before finding out.

Love is powerful. While we cannot predict whether we are over someone, there are steps you can take to communicate with your future partner about unresolved feelings.

QUESTION

SEVEN

—⊰⊱—

What are the things you wish you had told your younger self about relationships?

This is a maturity-based question. It provides insight into lessons learned and the willingness to apply those lessons. The Assured Dater is always attentive to patterns, lessons, and red flags. If you can answer this question honestly and insightfully, you are almost at the final stage of finding a positive relationship.

There will be a time when you meet someone and realize why all your past relationships didn't work out. This person will nurture what your younger self, current self, and future self need. And yes, I mentioned your younger self because it never truly dies. That's what most therapists refer to as the inner child.

I recently asked my insightful teenage male client this question after he had a difficult breakup with his girlfriend. With tears in his eyes, he told me that he wished he had told his younger self that love would hurt, but never to stop taking a chance on it. My mouth was wide open, and seeing him in pain over the loss of the relationship, I decided to ask him about his outlook on life. He explained that he had experienced the ups and downs of his parents' love and their constant willingness to support each other no matter what. He said that his parents had always taught him about the reality of love and the importance of finding someone mutually committed to working toward it. He then said, "You know what I learned from my ex?" "You cannot force someone to be that for you. They can either do that with you, or they are not."

This level of acceptance placed him at a different level of maturity that I had not observed in any older adult going through a divorce during my practice.

Another benefit of this question is understanding a person's current stage or their dating personality type.

If a person responds with superficial traits like, "I wish I had told my younger self to date someone with tons of money," or "I wish I had told my younger self that it is all about beauty," Again, these are exaggerated concepts. I genuinely hope you never meet anyone who answers this way, but if they do, examine what you want from the relationship.

EIGHT

What led to your last breakup?

When you ask this question, make sure the Law-and-Order intro song plays in your head. This is the ultimate interrogation technique in the early stages of dating. It's simple: your goal is to focus on the details, how the person responds, and look for any sign of accountability.

It's similar to a job interview when you're asked about your previous work experience. Future employers gather information to understand what to expect from you. If you were fired from your last position, they want to know why. Who was at fault? Are you accepting responsibility for your actions? Are you blaming your former employer? If you remain confrontational and bitter, they want to see if you've taken steps to correct the issues that led to your termination. This question requires careful analysis, but a good interviewer also pays attention to your non-verbal responses.

You question whether you've had a good conversation with your potential partner. Be mindful of energy shifts. Did they go from smiling to frowning? Did they suddenly cross their arms and bite their lips? Non-verbal cues reveal how much resentment persisted from the previous relationship and whether your potential partner has fully healed or is just covering it up.

If the response is, "I was cheated on," the follow-up question should be, "How did you find out you were cheated on?" This reveals how much healing the person still needs. If your potential partner says they found out from a friend or by spying on their phone, it could indicate they might have trouble trusting others in the future if they haven't fully healed.

There are many subjective responses to this question as well. If the person's response is, "I cheated," look for signs of remorse, accountability, willingness to accept the blame, and openness to be more honest and forthcoming in future relationships. If none of these are present, walk away!

If the person's response gears towards what the other person was not doing, "chores, household finances, etc.", know that this potential individual would have those expectations from you.

If the person responds with all fingers pointed towards their former partner, run! No matter how wrong a person in a relationship is, it takes two to tango. When I work with individuals going through a divorce or recent break-up, I realize healing begins with accountability for one's actions. That accountability may manifest as enabling behaviors or a lack of boundaries that lead to a person being treated in such a manner.

If the person responds with all fingers pointed towards themselves, run! Victim daters do this. Excessive accountability is also not a good sign. Willingness to take all the blame for the past relationship is a form of people-pleasing behavior. Balance is needed in the disbursement of accountability.

If the person responds with topics on domestic violence, be cautious! I cannot stress this enough. Statistically, a person who has been a victim of domestic violence is more likely to experience it again in their lifetime. You need to watch for certain patterns. This also applies to perpetrators of domestic violence. For example, Gus, a former Marine with severe PTSD, once engaged in physical acts against his ex-wife that he was not proud of. After sobering up, he attended several anger management classes and made a big turnaround. Sadly, his wife had given up on him and left with their child. His wife, Janet, started a new relationship six months later. Her new boyfriend had no history of domestic violence. However, because Janet was still unhealed from her trauma, it showed in her interactions; she would yell, scream, and taunt him into hitting her. It was only a matter of time before she struck him, and Chris reacted instinctively, without even realizing he was doing it. Janet's cycle of trauma continued. After ten years of chaos with Chris, she decided to return to her ex, Gus. He was the father of her children and had made a significant change in his attitude. But within less than six months of reuniting, Gus started drinking again, and their arguments grew more intense.

In this scenario, the only thing to blame is unhealed trauma. *Trauma sometimes causes us to perceive threats where they do not exist, which eventually creates a real threat we cannot deny.*

If Chris asked Janet this question, he would be sure to know that a therapist like me would recommend not to date anyone with a previous history of domestic violence as a victim or perpetrator until they have taken the time to heal in a therapeutic setting and have reached a higher level of emotional regulation. This would take at least one year, with advanced classes in domestic violence prevention and anger management training and an additional year to decompress from it all.

Breakup patterns are also a telltale of a person's dating style. If a person shows a pattern of breaking up for what are considered small reasons, there is a chance they are perfectionists and have difficulty committing. Gem Collectors and Royals are notorious for this.

If a person responds, "None of my exes have treated me right," there is a chance that they are victims. The question could always be, "Why?" It may throw the responder off guard, but the goal of the follow-up is to encourage the victim to take some ownership or responsibility. You do not want to be "captain-save-a-hoe"; you want to be able to push the individual into self-accountability.

QUESTION
NINE

---◦◦---

Which of your relationships changed your way of thinking in life, and how did that influence your thoughts on forgiveness?

If there's one thing my years of counseling have taught me, it's that everyone reaches enlightenment at different points in their lives.

Some relationships you experience will push you to grow, confront your inner demons, figure out precisely what you want in a person, realize your potential, and become unafraid to love fully. Ironically, many times it's a toxic relationship that helps a person get there. That's why I reassure my clients that sometimes, it takes the bad to recognize the good.

Again, if question eight was answered in detail, you will be able to identify which relationship changed your potential partner's thought process or if they are still stuck in a never-ending cycle of lessons unlearned.

The second part of this question is, how easy is it for you to forgive? Many couples therapists overlook this aspect of couples counseling. In most relationships, there is someone who can forgive and let go quickly, and others who will hold a twenty-five-year-old grudge like a mountain climber.

I find that individuals who hold grudges for an extended period are often anxious and driven, constantly reminding themselves of how they've been hurt to avoid being hurt again. The problem with this is that most people don't like when you hold on to the old version of themselves. Individuals who forgive and let things go are often vulnerable to exploitation. This individual typically is the Rescuer dating personality type.

Regardless of which side of the spectrum you're on, forgiveness is only essential if it has future boundaries. Boundaries are only necessary if there are consequences.

You can easily recognize people who hold grudges during the first few dates. They often talk about a long-lost friend, former spouse, or family member who wronged them. They tend to have a Victim personality and focus on how much they have been hurt repeatedly. Be cautious of a potential partner who constantly criticizes their ex, as they may have difficulty letting go.

QUESTION

TEN

When did you first become aware of your emotions?

This is a classic question about emotional intelligence. In therapy and assessment settings, I often ask clients to recall their earliest memories to understand the significant or traumatic memories that have stayed with them. A person's earliest memories usually influence whether they are driven by fear or joy.

In 2020, during the pandemic, I started my journey into private practice. Unbeknownst to me, the population I was about to work with would change forever. I launched a series of online campaigns to raise awareness about mental health, especially among men, who have an incredibly high mortality rate, including suicide, homicide, incarceration, and addiction. Through this campaign, I discovered through research that most men lack the emotional complexity needed to navigate life, let alone maintain healthy relationships.

The primary emotions I observed in men were anger and happiness. Anything else fits into either of those categories, which can make many men emotionally unavailable. This question also helps you avoid dating someone who is emotionally distant.

"Uh, I don't know" isn't a good response. Emotional awareness can help prevent inappropriate reactions to feelings. Some people confuse anger with sadness, while others mix sadness with depression. There's often confusion when I tell my clients that anger is a secondary emotion. However, when I started the exercise to identify the factors that lead to anger, we examined emotions such as frustration, embarrassment, loss of control, feeling overwhelmed, sadness, and irritability, among others. If you don't identify the primary emotion, you will only react to the typical signs of anger.

Emotions are the drive that determines how we respond to our environment.

The importance of emotional awareness is that I have met people in their forties who still don't understand their emotions. For example, it's common for the Obsessive dating personality type to be often unaware of their feelings and those of others, which can lead to controlling and explosive behaviors.

ELEVEN

———⚜———

How have your past
traumas shaped you?

This question doesn't mean you have to share your trauma with someone you've only gone on a few dates with. The goal is to see how emotionally aware your future partner is. Trauma plays a significant role in relationships. Childhood trauma often has predictable effects that influence future connections. For example, a child who experiences severe neglect and abandonment may grow up either fearing abandonment constantly or avoiding attachment altogether. Trauma can affect people in bipolar ways. In simple terms, the future might seem like a choice between black and white, hot and cold, or dark and light. As a therapist, I aim to help people who have experienced trauma find a balance in the gray area. For example, it's common for those who have been abused to become either very aggressive or extremely passive.

Fireworks and gunshots are examples I use in counseling to explain the difference between what is considered a threat and what isn't. For example, if your father hit you with a belt, seeing your partner holding a belt while talking to you could be a trigger, even if it's a harmless gesture. Teaching your brain to distinguish between what is a threat and what isn't is essential.

Among all these factors, my most consistent concern when counseling individuals who are moving toward a relationship is their trauma tolerance. In 2021, I met a coach who told me that, as someone raised in a strict, religious environment, her trauma tolerance was exceptionally high. She explained that because of this, she often tolerates more nonsense from partners than necessary. She mentioned that she sometimes forgives too easily because her partners never did anything worse than what she experienced in childhood. This led her to stay in relationships much longer than she should have, which, as a result, eroded her self-esteem and her ability to set clear boundaries with herself.

She told me that it was a struggle and that she had to go above and beyond to start cutting people off who added more trauma to her. You can see the hot-and-cold pattern in her statements because she either stays in an unhealthy relationship forever or cuts off someone at the slightest sign of imperfection. A person's trauma tolerance can determine how much crap they can handle.

Years ago, I decided to try out Tinder. OK, OK, I know. Tinder isn't a great place to find a potential partner, but it was a quick way to research what I was looking for. While exploring, I met many women who had severe histories of childhood abuse—sexually, emotionally, and physically. Most knew what I did for a living, so it wasn't unusual for them to share critical information so quickly.

It wasn't surprising to me when I realized that people who experienced severe childhood abuse often had long-term toxic relationships, either with one person or multiple individuals. This pattern was so typical that I couldn't ignore it. One woman I dated showed her fear of abandonment within the first two dates through obsessive phone calls. She sent multiple text messages within 20 seconds and constantly feared I would suddenly ghost her.

Her behavior reflected how she acted with her ex-boyfriend. It also came from her mother's sudden disappearance during her early years. I knew she couldn't overcome her fear. I could see she was trying, and I felt embarrassed that she couldn't stop herself from spiraling into multiple phone calls.

Another woman I dated experienced severe physical abuse from her stepfather while growing up. She initially told me that every relationship she had afterward was with an abusive man. She later confessed that a majority of the time, she was the aggressor. I understood that to keep myself safe, I needed to stay away until she had healed.

Another woman I dated experienced a different kind of trauma. She saw her father cheating on her mother multiple times and was forced to keep the secret. Her mother was very depressed and could barely get out of bed. Because of her mother's situation, she didn't want to make her depression worse by telling her that her teacher (the woman her father was cheating with) would sometimes visit her father's office. Over the years, she had several relationships but never fully committed to anyone. She became a Gem collector, paralyzed by fear of commitment and terrified of marrying a man like her father. During our first three dates, she avoided mentioning that she had cheated on multiple exes. I was fortunate enough to hear about it through the grapevine, which prompted me to ask more in-depth questions.

I'm telling you all this because I want you to understand that time matters. I could've wasted much of my life with these individuals, and I'd probably be paying the price now. Conversely, I could be lucky if they decided to heal while in a relationship with me. When deciding which you want to choose, the main question is, "If this person never changes, would I be able to tolerate this behavior for the rest of my life? Would I be able to tolerate his behavior for five, ten, or even twenty years?"

Figuring out your breaking point helps you understand how much you're willing to invest or how much you can handle. If you're aiming for a two-year relationship and know you can manage it for that long, go for it. If you're aiming for a six-month relationship and are confident you can handle the person for that period, go ahead. However, you should never lie to yourself about how long you can tolerate a potential partner's behavior. Again, time is precious.

In my practice, I consistently remind my clients to focus on what is real, rather than just potential. Anyone can have potential. A five-year-old might potentially become a doctor, but many factors must align for that to happen. Ironically, many people are dating and working toward building the most critical institution in life, yet they often focus on potential rather than the actual. For example, I've heard, "he has his mean ways, but I know he will get better." My response is, "OK. By the time he gets better, he would've caused you trauma."

If you want to grow in a company, you wouldn't choose one that says, "We appreciate your interest in joining us. However, we want to inform you that there may or may not be an opportunity for a promotion or raise...ever!" This is a significant red flag, and I urge every reader to approach relationships with the same caution as potential employment opportunities.

Everyone has faced some trauma; some people are aware of the impact the trauma has on them, and others are not. Some people do not experience side effects of trauma because of their strong support system, optimistic temperament, and spiritual backing.

What to look for when asking this question is someone thirsty to grow and heal and aware enough not to let their trauma disrupt your peace. Regardless of the severity of the trauma, you want to be with

35

someone who says, "I want to take control of my life. I do not want my trauma to take control of me." Until you find that person, you're better off alone because some individuals are comfortable in the chaos and toxicity. Some individuals are comfortable never growing. Pay attention.

Another kind of trauma that many people don't talk about is financial trauma. Growing up in poverty can lead individuals to develop a complex relationship with money, either by overspending and being careless with their finances or by becoming financial hoarders. A person's relationship with money reveals a lot, as it is a key predictor of whether a relationship will last. This is serious. It's something that should be a priority from the start. If your potential partner has bad spending habits, consider walking away. Please don't assume they will change unless you see genuine efforts toward better financial stability. In this case, ensuring the person has good credit, minimal debt, a spending plan, and skills in finding bargains is crucial. I don't believe anyone needs to be perfect. You shouldn't waste time with someone who isn't trying to improve, or you'll end up dealing with a problem you didn't cause.

A couple is the foundation on which our society is built. If a couple functions well, there will be positive results for future generations. This is one of the reasons I always tell my clients who have marital issues that their marriage is not about them; it is about generations to come. I remind them that whatever is done will be remembered for eternity and future generations. This is why dating should never be taken lightly.

A Nigerian proverb states: "The eyes that will take you to your old age will not start causing you problems when you're young." Meaning, pay attention to problems while you're young so you won't regret ignoring them.

A person's trauma is also a predictor of several factors. A popular trauma testing tool has proven to indicate not only future mental health circumstances but also physical health outcomes because of trauma. The Adverse Childhood Experience Survey (ACES) questionnaire has revealed various factors and traumas that a child may encounter. For instance, Individuals who experience PTSD or anxiety have a higher likelihood of developing heart conditions or high blood pressure. Understanding a person's trauma is crucial for gaining a deeper understanding of their experiences. Ensure that anyone you're involved with is self-aware and committed to their healing journey. You do not want to be with someone who does not recognize or cannot acknowledge their issues. It will be highly frustrating throughout the relationship to help them understand.

Rob, a businessman and multi-millionaire, was the sweetest talker you could ever meet. This man always knew how to sell water to those with functioning taps. He sold sand to people in the desert and salt water to those on boats in the ocean. Rob was genuinely a lovely man. However, his trauma haunted him in ways he couldn't understand. In his childhood, his father, also a businessman, became addicted to gambling and alcohol. On the outside, they appeared to be the perfect family, but inside, his mother constantly worried that his father's impulsive actions would drive the whole family into bankruptcy. Rob's father was the type of person who would buy a BMW just because it was Friday; his impulsive spending usually happened when he was drunk. Sometimes, he would skimp on bills just for the emotional high of gambling. Rob's parents never divorced, and fortunately, they never went bankrupt. When Rob began dating, it wasn't surprising that many women he surrounded himself with were drawn to his money. He didn't have the best looks, and sweet talk was not his strong suit.

Over time, he realized these women were using him and made a conscious decision to change. Unfortunately, the change he wanted was not for the better. Rob realized the power of alcohol, and soon, one week before he planned to marry, he recognized he couldn't stop drinking. Everything he had achieved in life, he attributed to the courage that alcohol gave him; his wife, his kids, his job, his businesses, and his confidence were all intertwined with alcohol. His wife struggled to understand this because Rob's family always appeared perfect on the outside. But soon after saying 'I do,' she began to notice patterns in Rob that suggested he was not going to become a high-functioning alcoholic or gambler like his father. Rob was more impulsive and spoiled. Financial trauma and the indirect trauma of watching his father drink himself into a stupor affected him deeply. She was pregnant with twins when she considered leaving Rob. The entirety of their relationship was affected by Rob's issues, and his wife's tolerance of trauma was influenced by her past; she had watched her father behave similarly. With this background, she knew how to handle Rob, but only in an enabling way. Understanding trauma tolerance goes both ways. You're not asking this question to point fingers at others or to say, 'Hey, you're bad.' You're asking this question to understand how you might contribute to another person's trauma.

TWELVE

What are your friends like?

The interesting part of this question is that you can observe your potential partner's friends without asking. However, if you want to understand more before the third date, just watching might not be enough. Most people don't meet their partner's friends by the third date.

Gentlemen, the woman you're about to date has a board of directors that must vote on whether you're compatible with her. Her board may include her high school best friend, college best friend, and sometimes her mother, sister, or a colleague's best friend. Unsurprisingly, one of the most famous quotes that has transcended generations is, "Show me your friends, and I will tell you who you are."

Albert Bandura proposed the social learning theory, which explains that people learn by observing and imitating the behaviors of others, especially those they perceive as credible or successful. That's why it's essential to observe what your potential partner's friends are like and how much they look up to their friends.

Jared pledged to a fraternity during his first year of college, and everything he did revolved around it. Every graduation ceremony, guys' trip, barbecue, attitude toward employment, and dating centered on his fraternity. Jean, however, was the opposite. She had two friends from kindergarten who were already married by the time she met Jared. They spent a lot of time on the phone but rarely met in person during the first three weeks of dating. Jean and Jared recognized their differing priorities. Jared and his friends valued fun and constantly sought new experiences, while Jean and her friends emphasized stability and consistency. Ninety percent of Jared's friends were single bachelors uninterested in commitment, making Jared the anomaly in the group. It was common for Jared to face teasing from his friends when he chose to spend the weekend with Jean. Over time, a tug-of-war emerged as Jean began to insist on feeling prioritized, a demand fueled by her "board of directors," who wanted Jean's relationship to mirror their own.

Two factors influence this situation. Your future partner's past will always impact their present. People carry an established cultural framework into relationships. Ideally, you can find someone whose previous experiences match the kind of life you're aiming to build, but that's not always possible. Additionally, many friends struggle to accept that change is natural, and most fail to see the importance of maintaining a balance—you can dedicate time to your friends, partner, or both at once. There's often a lingering fear of losing the friendship dynamic once someone in the group starts a serious relationship. It's common for everyone in the group to resist change, especially when people are at different stages of life.

In Jared and Jean's situation, discussing expectations can clarify individuals' introverted and extroverted needs.

Four reasons why knowing your future partner's friend circle matters.

- **To understand how strong their support system is:** Your future partner's support also counts as part of your support system. For example, if you need help moving, your partner's friends might step in. Since the pandemic, the average American has fewer close friends. Having a strong support network provides a sense of safety and assistance.
- **To understand the behavior your future partner may show:** if your girlfriend's friends are disrespectful and she acts the same way, they probably share similar traits due to learned behaviors. If your boyfriend's friends are habitual cheaters, don't be surprised if he behaves likewise. While not everyone mirrors their friends' actions, noticing these patterns can provide a better understanding. Cassandra, a left-wing Democrat, met Chris at a party. The two

instantly fell in love and avoided politics in their conversations. Christopher's friends were right-wing Republicans and didn't hide it. A barbecue at Christopher's friend's house revealed all she needed to know. She wasn't surprised when she visited his home for the first time and saw that everything Christopher did aligned with right-wing views. This helped them discuss key parts of their future relationship.

- **To understand who can be your ally:** your partner's friends may help you discover who your partner is and assist you during a relationship crisis. An ally is essential because it can provide insights you might not grasp. Julie cried multiple times when James would shut down for a week without communicating with her, then return as if nothing had happened. She did not know what to do. She was sure he was not cheating because he hardly left the house. Julie often felt she had done something wrong and began walking on eggshells, but after a few months, James repeated the same behavior. One day, Julie seized the chance to ask one of James's friends about this behavior. James's friend laughed and said, "Oh, you're experiencing the James moment." Confused, she asked, " What? " James's friend explained that James struggled with a mild form of bipolar disorder (Cyclothymic Disorder) and had random periods of depression. James's friend advised her to visit him during these moments, but to avoid being overbearing, as James used this time to recharge. Julie was relieved that she had not overreacted.

- **To determine who can serve as your model couple:** In my career as a couple's counselor, I've found that couples with successful role models tend to fare better. Remember, we are always operating under the principles of social learning theory.

- **To know what your partner considers fun:** planning a surprise party is more straightforward with your future partner's friends. Help is always a call away, especially on your first birthday as a couple.

- **To find out which friends can get along with your future partner's friend:** Life is much easier when both you and your partner's friends can get along. Game nights run smoother, and guess what? You may be able to find a future partner for your friends within the friend group.

THIRTEEN

What emotions do you struggle with feeling and expressing?

This two-part question carries more weight than a trailer full of concrete. Of course, this also depends on question eleven. In my experience, this is exactly how you figure out the type of person you are dating. Gem collectors typically lack the patience for these questions. They want to get in and out quickly. Gem collectors tend to avoid emotions and often give shallow responses. Therefore, questions ten, eleven, twelve, and thirteen are typically used to determine if someone is serious.

Emotion is energy in motion. While some individuals can identify and respond to emotions, others simply react, which indicates unhealed trauma, lack of self-awareness, and unhinged impulsivity. Ironically, I find both men and women guilty of this, contributing to the four horsemen of the apocalypse described by John Gottman.

In his research with couples, John Gottman found that couples at risk of breakup or divorce often show one of four emotional responses: criticism (constantly pointing out negatives), defensiveness (being overly guarded even when not under attack), stonewalling (shutting down emotional responses to provoke your partner, intentionally or not), and contempt (a nonverbal sign of disdain for your partner). All four responses typically indicate ineffective communication and low emotional intelligence, as feelings and expressions can differ.

Jake, a middle-aged man, responded, "I struggle with expressing and feeling anger." He explained that his primary fear was losing complete control due to several instances from his childhood when he had. This made Jake an "Imploder. "

I always tell my clients that I am more afraid of imploders than exploders. Exploders (those with the Bulls fighting style) are predictable, and you can always tell what will set them off, while imploders are vipers who can go off at any moment. Jake realized this about himself and developed a habit of bottling up his emotions because he feared showing them.

In a counseling session, I told Jake that anger is not always a destructive emotion. Anger can be beneficial when used in moderation and a controlled manner. Showing anger is something learned from the media, family, and friends. Jake understood this right after I said it. With his deep voice, he learned how to express his feelings during an argument without yelling, breathe slowly to calm his heartbeat, and stay grounded by naming items in his environment to prevent himself from blacking out. In simple terms, he learned a diplomatic way to argue.

On the other hand, some people feel guilty when they are happy. These individuals come from emotionally distant households characterized by absent or emotionally distant parents. These parents expect children who are workaholics (i.e., children who constantly do chores, homework, or extracurricular activities), with limited social and emotional outlets, and who are taught that productivity is essential, and are made to feel guilty for having too much fun.

Tracy, an Asian immigrant, grew up in a household where life centered around running a business. She was expected to attend school, do chores, work in the family shop, participate in extracurricular activities, and follow a curfew at 8 pm (the same time the store closed). Her "birds and the bees" talk was full of threats of shame if she ever got a boyfriend. To restrict Tracy's freedom, she was never given a car; when she finally got one, it was covered with the shop's logo. Tracy's puberty was full of anxiety, driven by comments like, "You have nothing to complain about. You have a much better life than we did in the sixties." Whenever Tracy found something that made her happy, it was criticized with remarks like, "Oh, that's horrible music," "Don't wear that; it is too revealing," or "Makeup is for women who are looking for the wrong attention." She never kept up with the latest trends in anything.

At 21, she explored the vibrant city life after graduating from college in her hometown. For the first time, she felt like a free woman and embraced it fully. Parties—clubs and more parties. She had friends of all races and traveled to as many places as her new job and graduate program allowed. Still, partying felt like guilt—it seemed like a waste of time, and she found herself compensating by studying and working more. This strained her relationships. "Loosen up" became the theme of the argument because she wanted, more than anything, to be productive. Happiness is about letting go of social norms.

Anyone can struggle with an emotion because emotions are often connected to memories, and some of these memories can be unpleasant. If something terrible happened the last time you felt happy, that happiness may never feel the same again. If sadness came from a heavy loss, you might feel the need to chase happiness at all costs, which can also be risky. Emotions play a crucial role in every conversation about future relationships.

FOURTEEN

What are the steps you've taken to overcome your trauma?

The answer to this will demonstrate enlightenment and reveal a person's healing journey. Like the previous QUESTION, if someone has a history of financial trauma, you need to see them in a space of financial empowerment or actively working on S.M.A.R.T goals toward that.

If a person has a history of sexual trauma, you need to see them demonstrate clear body boundaries, and you will need to foster a sense of sexual safety around them through intentional consent.

If someone has a history of physical trauma, watch how they act when angry. Also, note that sudden movements during an argument can trigger a traumatic response such as fight, flight, freeze, or fawn. Physical trauma often repeats itself based on social learning theory, meaning hurt people can hurt others, while healed people can help others heal.

If someone has a history of emotional trauma, you need to assess whether they have a secure sense of self. Please pay close attention to the narratives they tell themselves. This means they must show that their self-perception is not based on what was said to them in childhood.

For this section, I will provide an example. Jackie grew up with a hyper-critical mother who was a perfectionist. Jackie's mother wanted her to be slim and girly so every man could desire her. She would point out parts of Jackie's body that she disliked, doing so repeatedly throughout her childhood. In adulthood, Jackie spends more time criticizing her body than her mother. This has affected every relationship because she would be hyper-critical towards her partner or attract someone as hyper-critical as her mother.

The hyper-critical attitude of her mother became part of her daily routine, and she couldn't shake off negative comments or intrusive thoughts at any time. This led to anorexic and bulimic behaviors. Jackie would either starve herself or purge whenever she felt she had overeaten. She also exercised excessively to ensure she didn't gain a pound. Ironically, Jackie also employed the same hyper-critical approach with her daughter, perpetuating the cycle.

I am focusing on emotional abuse because it is less likely to be acknowledged. Physical abuse and sexual abuse are observable. Emotional abuse is internal.

You also need to be cautious of those with false healing stories. For example, someone who claims that all past trauma disappeared after just one therapy session, watching a documentary, or reading a book is simply lying. Complex trauma is an ongoing process that requires consistency and multiple approaches to healing. If someone doesn't realize that financial trauma can be persistent and believes that just creating a budget means they've moved past it, that isn't true.

Many people get stuck on the surface and rely on religion, drugs, or a party lifestyle to heal. That's an unrealistic goal. On the opposite end, some may go overboard with their healing by visiting monasteries, trying psychedelics, undergoing therapy, using psychotropic medications, or natural remedies while excessively exploring different methods. Obsessively focusing on healing can be a red flag masked by good intentions. Trust your instincts. You want someone comfortable with themselves, confident, and willing to create a positive space to be with you.

FIFTEEN

What does it look like when you're angry, and how does it influence your fighting style?

I am always astonished when I hear that many people don't discuss this. Arguments and conflicts are a standard part of every relationship. We cannot avoid them, no matter how much we try. Think about it: Your relationship with your favorite sibling is probably good in your adult life because you fought a lot, and in the process, you learned to be with each other and understand each other. Fights are going to happen; what matters is fighting fairly.

You need to understand what your potential partner is like when angry. I would not recommend committing to a relationship with anyone until you see how they act when upset. Unfortunately, many people put their best foot forward in the first few days of a relationship, which doesn't give us a clear sense of their behavior when they are angry. However, there are other ways to gauge how your partner is or will be when upset. For instance, please pay attention to their body language when the waitress gets their order wrong. Pay attention to signs of unnecessary road rage.

It is safe to say that simply asking your partner, "What are you like when you're angry?" will not give you a proper understanding of their anger. What you need to focus on is their body language. Is your potential partner comfortable discussing their emotions? Is your potential partner aware that anger is a secondary emotion? These are critical points to consider because many people who don't recognize that anger is a secondary emotion tend to be very destructive to themselves or others when angry.

Recognizing anger as a secondary emotion provides insight into its underlying causes, such as embarrassment, frustration, sadness, and other often-overlooked emotions, including jealousy.

Some people express their anger outwardly, while others keep their feelings bottled up. Knowing how a person gets angry will help you identify their fighting style. It's essential to have a partner who feels comfortable expressing their emotions appropriately, regardless of the circumstances.

Also, try to determine what type of person you're dealing with. Is this person verbally aggressive when angry? Is this person physically aggressive when angry? Is this person aggressive toward the environment, throwing things when angry? You need to know these things; you do not want to waste your time with someone who cannot express their emotions effectively. If you are still reading this book, I hope you understand that spending time with someone with whom you must walk on eggshells is not helpful for your physical and emotional health.

Another reason to ask this question is to understand your potential partner's coping skills. Some people prefer going for walks, punching a punching bag, reading a book, journaling, or engaging in other activities that help take their mind off the situation. Knowing your potential partner's coping skills when they are angry is essential so that when you find yourself in a similar situation, you can support them in reinforcing those skills, e.g., encouraging them to take a walk or engage in any of the other activities mentioned.

This question also raises a secondary question: What signs indicate that you are angry? In 2013, I took a course in anger management to help my clients. This course emphasized understanding the initial signs of anger through your body's physical sensations. Upon exploring this, I realized that everyone has an anger thermometer. Each person's threshold is different, and each person's point of no return varies. If someone is unaware of their initial anger cues, they haven't attained the emotional maturity necessary to maintain a healthy relationship. Determine if your partner's early signs include sweating, jitteriness, a pounding heart, dilated pupils, or stuttering. If you can identify these signs, you can prevent a potentially volatile situation from escalating rapidly.

I'm not saying you should not date anyone who gets angry; that's unrealistic. However, you certainly want to avoid dating someone with a history of being abusive or whose fighting style doesn't align with yours. Don't expose yourself to trauma.

You've learned about love languages, and this book will now explore fighting styles. I've noticed that a person's fighting style often correlates with their emotional intelligence. Here, I've compiled six main fighting styles that I have observed in couples.

- **The Volcano:** Those with the volcano fighting style tend to pile up emotions like a hoarder on steroids. Nothing is forgiven; their lack of reaction is usually because "it is not the right time or space" to explode. Volcanoes are masters of keeping score, doing so both consciously and unconsciously. There is usually no warning sign that a Volcano is about to explode. A key characteristic of the Volcano is its inability to recognize safe spaces to express intense emotions. The Volcano is usually afraid of its own emotions. Hence, they ignore problems until they can no longer ignore them, and then the feared outcome occurs (an unimaginable explosion). After the explosion, there is usually shame and guilt, which leads to the Volcano being overly apologetic or overly permissive until the subsequent explosion erupts. Until Volcanoes realize that conflict needs to be addressed assertively and immediately, the cycle usually continues.

- **The Jester:** The Jester makes jokes to calm situations by laughing them off. The Jester is passive-aggressive and employs a great deal of sarcasm that can either escalate tensions or mitigate them. The Jester can be annoying because serious situations call for serious responses. However, serious responses from the Jester usually mean you've taken it too far. If you're with a Jester, remember that laughing is their way of coping. They are not trying to annoy you. The harder they laugh, the more dangerous things may become if pushed too far.

- **The Snake:** Snakes are sneaky, quiet, and skilled predators because they have mastered the ability to avoid triggering all five senses of their prey. They are calculatedly aggressive. They watch you, give subtle warnings, and then strike precisely. The Snake is spiteful and doesn't hurt in the most obvious way. For instance, The Snake might suddenly forget to fill your gas tank because they are upset you didn't cook for them. The snake may spread a rumor about you and be as curious as you are about discovering who started it. The snake is unpredictable and slick. The snake is a master of sneaky insults and will throw a slight jab at a core event of your life and then retreat like it did not happen. The snake may damage your relationship with another person as a form of punishment for what you did to them. The snake never forgets; they wait for an opportunity to pay you back for the hurt you caused. If you've ever watched Game of Thrones, Littlefinger is an example of a snake. He never got his hands dirty but used conflicts with others to his advantage.

- **The Peacekeeper:** This is a master of conflict avoidance. The peacekeeper's goal is to maintain peace, even if it means fighting within themselves. They are addicted to ignoring issues until they become too obvious to overlook. The danger of being with a peacekeeper is that people often confuse them with the Desperate dating personality type. Peacekeepers understand the nature of war and have learned that no one truly wins, which is why they can be dangerous fighters when their backs are against the wall.

- **The Bull:** This individual is determined to fight no matter what and exemplifies stubbornness. Bulls are willing to fight anywhere, anytime, and for any reason. They dislike being messed with. Bulls tend to make as much of a scene as possible during fights, with no regard for tactics or fairness. When a bull is upset, everyone notices, and it's best to stay away. Living with a bull is like living with a ticking time bomb. You know it is guaranteed to explode, sometimes, even before the time is up. Bulls tend to intimidate before the escalation of things. Bulls do not mind being hurt if it means you will hurt too.

- **The Diplomat:** The Diplomat's fighting style revolves around skilled communication, negotiation, and emotional intelligence. The diplomat avoids criticism, contempt, stonewalling, and defensiveness in everyday relationship discussions. The diplomat is different from the peacekeeper. The diplomat fights fairly after making multiple attempts to communicate. The diplomat can make deals during conflicts to help ease the situation. The diplomat is also very calculated and knows when to walk away from situations that no longer serve them. Diplomats are realistic about their goals for resolving conflicts. Therefore, if a diplomat realizes that a relationship will always be filled with conflict, they will walk away without looking back.

Emotional intelligence influences an individual's fighting style. Therefore, in the dating scene, it's essential to consider these factors to understand what you're getting into. For example, a bull and a peacekeeper will drive themselves crazy just as much as a bull and another bull. If you have done the work this book provides, your lifelong fighting style will be that of a Diplomat.

QUESTION
SIXTEEN

What is it like when you're stressed?

Stress is a common experience. In today's world, we're constantly busy. Between work, family, life, friends, finances, medical issues, and mental health concerns, there are many sources of stress. Some people manage stress well and avoid bringing it into other areas of their lives. Some can be stressed at work but not carry it home. Others might be stressed at home, but they do not let it affect their work. And some struggle with both. It's essential to find out if your potential partner can tell the difference between stress levels and unrelated circumstances, so they don't take work stress out on you. Asking this question also helps the person gain insight into themselves.

A follow-up question is: What are the signs that you're stressed? Again, you need to see relationships as potential business partnerships. You need to see relationships as a means of understanding and growing together. Knowing your partner's stress level will help you take steps to alleviate it, rather than exacerbate it.

Janet, a multiracial woman, grew up in an environment filled with constant stress. Her mother was always burned out, and her father was constantly worn out. They were almost always late for everything—living in New York City didn't make it easier. Interestingly, Janet later realized that most of her parents' stress was self-inflicted. They would wake up late and make breakfast, which made them late for scheduled activities. This poor time management habit rubbed off on Janet, making her the same way.

A year before entering a serious relationship, Janet couldn't shake off the stress that accompanied each of her partnerships. Since feeling overwhelmed was part of her daily life, she constantly procrastinated until the last minute. Sadly, whenever she was stressed, she took it out on those around her, even though she knew it was self-inflicted. Chris, her fiancé, was the complete opposite. His laid-back attitude only increased her stress. She found herself worried about what to wear, the bills, and practically everything else.

This might be an extreme example of stress, but it's essential to understand what triggers stress in a potential partner. Are they able to recognize what they can and cannot control? Can they manage what they can and let go of what they cannot? Ninety percent of the conflicts I saw in couples counseling revolved around these issues. One partner gets stressed over chores, while the other doesn't; one worries about bills, and the other is unaffected. This cycle of stress often leads the stressed individual to feel unnoticed or unheard.

Everyone has a different stress response, and your goal is to understand your potential partner's stress response and help them reflect on their stress response in various past situations. Don't waste time.

SEVENTEEN

❖

What is your relationship with drugs and alcohol?

I am going to enjoy this QUESTION. In 2017, I obtained my certificate in alcohol and drug counseling. This was my first certificate outside of my professional therapist's license. To obtain the certificate, I learned a lot about the stages of drug and alcohol use. To keep it brief and straightforward, I'll review it quickly. There are four stages of addiction. The first stage is *use.* In this stage, the individual occasionally drinks in social situations and has no addiction or attachment to the substance. The second stage is *misuse;* in this stage, the individual uses the substance for a reason, such as being angry, sad, wanting something to have fun, or wanting something to help them calm down. I refer to this stage as the self-medication stage. The individual uses the substance to cope with emotions; eventually, those emotions become attached to the need for the substance. For instance, many marijuana smokers say, " I want to feel calm, so let me take a joint. " The third stage is called the *abuse* stage. In this stage, the individual takes more of the substance than needed. For example, one shot turns into a whole bottle of liquor. The last stage is called the *dependency* stage. The individual is physiologically dependent on the substance and cannot go a day without it without experiencing withdrawal symptoms. The dependency stage is critical for many people, especially those who drink alcohol. Suddenly quitting could lead to catastrophic consequences.

This question is essential to ask your potential partner because many people use substances without realizing their level of addiction. Additionally, many hide the fact that they are in active recovery. Recovery occurs when someone chooses to stop using substances like alcohol, opiates, or cocaine because they harm their life. The recovery process is rigorous and should not be taken lightly, as those in recovery face a daily risk of relapse, which can lead to binge behaviors. This is important to keep in mind when considering a potential partner.

I spent two and a half years of my career working in local outpatient rehab, and I used to play this fun game called Hot Seat. In the hot seat, I invite a client to sit in the middle of the group, and everyone in the group must ask the client a question. The questions ranged from simple to difficult. In this exercise, I noticed something. Whenever clients faced the question of dating, there was always resistance about whether it was OK to tell a potential partner that they were in active addiction or recovery. In group counseling sessions, I always emphasize the importance of being fully transparent with a potential partner if there is any form of addiction. You must be transparent because you don't want your future partner to waste their time. Your future partner also needs to understand what could jeopardize your recovery.

This true story is one of the most heart-wrenching stories in this book. Rachel, a beautiful woman in her prime, finally met the man of her dreams and was determined to settle down. Rachel would have bottles of wine and liquor on hand whenever they had parties at her house, and noticed Charles always refused to drink but never fully explained why, besides saying, "I don't want to drink." Over time, she noticed that he became bothered by her drinking. He would make passive-aggressive statements like, "Oh, you're just going to drink all that?" Charles never talked about why alcohol affected him, and Rachel concluded with her friends that he was just a "Debbie Downer".

All he had to do was tell her that he was in recovery, but he was terrified she would abandon him. He was also scared that she would no longer want to be with him if she learned the things alcohol made him do. So, like anyone would, he kept it to himself. Charles would attend 12-step meetings immediately after work and lie about going grocery shopping. This stigma was powerful for him. He never once brought his recovery coins into the house. Out of rebellion, Rachel started drinking outside the home because she knew her partner disliked it. This made him more resentful. One day, Rachel got into a car accident, leading to complaints that resulted in her use of medication.

Rachel, like most people addicted to any substance, took her opiate pills religiously and gradually needed more. Her addiction changed. Six months after being prescribed opiate pain pills, she realized she couldn't go a day without them without feeling sick. She never told Charles and kept it to herself. Her doctor started to suspect her addiction and stopped prescribing the pills, which led her to a friend who sold her the pills and eventually convinced her to try heroin because it was cheaper. Rachel knew she was addicted but didn't want to tell her partner.

After losing her job, she began to act strangely to satisfy her cravings. She became distant. Charles sensed that something was wrong and believed the only way to reconnect with Rachel was to drink with her occasionally. Their bond started to recover, and she began to enjoy staying at home, leading to more conversations between them. Initially, he tried to limit her alcohol intake, but gradually, he started to lose control. The alcohol addiction was unlike any other, and soon, violence broke out. Throughout all this, Charles never wanted to be her hero. As domestic violence worsened, Rachel's need for substances increased, and she started stealing from him, which caused more fights. One day, he came into the apartment with two bottles of whiskey, ready to drink with her, and found her lying on the floor—she had overdosed on fentanyl. His journey to recovery from this was lifelong, and I hope no one has to go through it. They never discussed drugs and alcohol openly. The secrecy ultimately led to their downfall.

Statistically speaking, one in four individuals will be addicted to a substance at some point in their lives. This is not a conversation to avoid; it needs to be had. Rachel would have survived if she had asked for help. Openness to discussing addiction may have helped them address things differently.

In my time working as an alcohol and drug counselor, I have heard many stories like this—One partner is addicted, and the other partner does not know. Addiction thrives in isolation. The more secrets you can keep about your addiction, the stronger the addiction becomes. Talk to your potential partner about drugs and alcohol.

Another reason to do so is to understand the history of substances they have used and what their needs are. If someone is in recovery, it is best to wait at least two years before getting into a relationship, based on my professional experience.

In summary, this question isn't just about discovering what substances your potential partner uses, but also whether they use them to cope with something. Its goal is to evaluate their stage of addiction and whether you can handle their substance use. During a date, observe how many drinks they have, their eye movements, frequency of bathroom trips, and sniffing. If there are signs of addiction, don't ignore them; they indicate a problem. Make sure you're not contributing to addiction by encouraging it or giving money for it. People hurt others. Don't waste your time.

Addiction to substances is not always visible on a person's face. Someone can appear professional and organized while still struggling with some form of addiction. Not everyone fits the stereotype of an "addict".

EIGHTEEN

What do you think would cause our breakup if it were to happen?

Question to ask on the third date. By your third date, you should be able to identify all the red flags based on the questions in this book. One reason for asking this question is to gauge a person's level of insight into the relationship that is beginning to develop. For instance, if you dislike how someone chews when eating food, it is essential not to ignore it because you'll likely share meals with that person for the rest of your life.

Asking this question to your future partner will give you an idea of whether they pay attention to the same things, too. You also want to ask this question to let the other person inquire about your understanding of the pros and cons of a potential relationship that you can explore to see what you can and cannot handle.

Again, what I have learned as a therapist is that what a person dislikes and ignores at the beginning of the relationship is often what they will have to deal with for the rest of their lives and may ultimately lead to a breakup.

Kathy, a real estate agency director, earns over six figures. She meets Blake, a laid-back man comfortable with an average salary. He possesses all the positive qualities she desires in a partner. However, Kathy cannot stand Blake's sixty-thousand-a-year salary. To combat this, she weighed her options to identify other positive traits: he is good with children, has supportive friends, is emotionally intelligent, is moderately ambitious, and takes his mental health seriously. All the negatives revolve around his job: he barely has enough time to take off on a trip, and she has to refrain from asking for expensive things to protect his pride. One day, Blake asked Kathy what might lead to their breakup, and Kathy responded, "The fact that you don't make enough money, and I have to be cautious about how I flaunt my money in front of you." Although Blake did not care about their financial differences, her words planted a seed in his mind, and he began to notice her affinity for luxury items.

It is essential to ask this question to give your partner insight into areas that could be improved. Once again, my favorite thing to do with clients who meet someone with long-term potential is to ask: If your potential partner never changed over the next 2 to 15 years, would you be able to handle it? Why? It's easy to deal with things you're not comfortable with during the honeymoon phase of a relationship. The love hormones and dopamine chemicals released during that time are designed to cloud your judgment. You need to know if those red flags will be tolerable once the cloud lifts.

Another example is Benjamin, a classy man from an upper-middle-class background who had the opportunity to travel internationally, attend private schools, and enjoy the benefits of being surrounded by the wealthy. Benjamin's favorite place to go was a coffee shop near his job.

Benjamin loved many things, but nothing he loved more than a good cup of coffee, a tasty pastry, and a peaceful atmosphere to relax in on a Saturday morning. Hence, a frequent visit to a local coffee shop. He met a woman named Linda and realized that she was more than just a server; she could engage in high-level intellectual conversations on any topic and was more engaging than anyone he worked with. Four months after their frequent weekly chit-chats, Benjamin gathered the courage to give her his number, and soon they started dating. Benjamin became a classic sculptor and began to spend money on her to help her dress like the people he spent his social gatherings with. Linda expressed her need to be accepted for who she was. In this context, it is safe to say that Benjamin was a Sculptor.

After five dates, Benjamin finally met Linda's family. He was not impressed. Benjamin didn't like his future mother-in-law's attitude towards life. It was unsettling. Benjamin could overlook that she came from a lower-income family, but he couldn't ignore how her family behaved during their engagement party. Despite this, Benjamin chose to marry Linda out of love. Planning the wedding became stressful because Benjamin felt ashamed of Linda's family. He secretly hoped for a destination wedding so Linda's family wouldn't be able to afford to attend.

Linda noticed Benjamin's attitude toward her family but chose to ignore it, hoping he would eventually get used to them as he had to her. One day, after a conversation, Benjamin admitted how much he disliked being around Linda's family and expressed things Linda could no longer ignore. She was shocked by this, saw a different side of him, and quickly labeled him a classist. When they tried to work things out, Linda asked him a question, and once again, Benjamin confessed that if they broke up, it would be because their future kids would be around her family. Linda ended the engagement.

Don't be shy about what you can't handle. If you can't manage something about your future partner, let them go before things get too deep. Unfortunately, many people have what I call "potential syndrome." They ignore the face value of what's in front of them for the potential that the person will eventually become their ideal partner. If you can't handle it now, there's a good chance you won't be able to handle it later.

NINETEEN

———— ✦≪◦≫✦ ————

What's the first thing you thought when you saw me?

Ever heard of love at first sight? It feels like bliss and a deep sense of euphoria. However, it is essential to recognize that various psychological and biological principles are at work when you meet someone and feel an immediate attraction. To give you a quick lesson, pheromones play a key role in attraction. Factors that contribute to attraction include facial symmetry, waist-to-hip ratio in women, voice, hair texture, skin tone, scent, and more. Love at first sight is more profound than you might think. Genetically speaking, humans transmit information through pheromones that indicate reproductive capability. For more information, watch "The Science of Sex Appeal," a documentary that explores the science behind attraction.

Asking this question can give you insight into what your potential partner desires. If someone is overly focused on your body, it might mean they are more interested in passion and erotic lovemaking. If they are excessively drawn to your personality, it suggests that your traits either fulfill something they lack or reinforce something they already have. If a person mainly focuses on their career, it indicates a need for financial security. Understanding what the person thought when they first saw you is essential.

Science indicates that physical attraction leads human beings to interact with one another, after which all the other factors come into play. That is true.

However, some people I have met insist that physical attraction was and will never be a factor in determining their reasons for being in a relationship. If that's you, that's OK. What needs to happen is an analysis of how people perceive you.

Again, you might be dating multiple people during your dating phase. Analyzing what others see when they first encounter you reveals a lot. I once met a woman who struggled to understand why men sexualized her. She was a voluptuous woman who was highly attractive. No matter how much she tried to downplay her allure to ward off unwanted men, she always seemed to attract men who were Gem collectors or Rescuers.

I gave her therapeutic homework: to ask every man she dated in the next six months this question. There was consistency in all the answers. The men usually responded with, "I thought you were very hot." After further explanation from these men, she began to understand the impression she was giving off. Many men told her she had a serious damsel-in-distress vibe. This persona attracted men even more because they felt the need to save her. This vibe aligns with the principles outlined in The Law of Attraction, which explains how people attract things. Men who see helplessness, especially those who are financially stable but emotionally unstable, found her highly attractive. They obsessively showed off their finances by giving lavish gifts and traveling to make her happy.

Because she understood what men initially thought of her when they first saw her, she began to portray herself as a more confident and self-reliant woman. She worked on her passions and businesses, creating plans to ensure her bills were paid from her resources. She did not ignore the gifts men gave her; instead, she consistently made it a point to show that she had more than enough to spare. This significantly diminished her damsel-in-distress vibe and soon transformed how she presented herself and dressed. She was determined to convey a woman who would not tolerate nonsense from anyone, having realized what people thought of her at first glance.

In the dating game, you must choose someone who recognizes you for who you are, not what you are pretending to be. Therefore, if what they like about you is who you're pretending to be, you know where the relationship stands.

TWENTY

What made you keep responding to the flirt's text messages or calls?

Everyone connects in different ways. Some meet at work, while others meet online. Some meet through friends, and others through family. Regardless of how you meet, there's initial attraction, and then there's what keeps that attraction going. People usually don't keep responding to texts and calls from someone they're not interested in. It's essential to learn what keeps someone's interest alive. For instance, if you meet someone online, the fact that you didn't meet in person means much of the information you use to build attraction comes from pictures and profiles, which can be full of lies. When texting, calling, or FaceTiming someone, you can start to see what is false and what is real over time by asking the questions in this book. Dating is a skill that needs to be developed to find the right person. Learning these cues will help you understand what keeps a person interested or what sparks their initial interest.

Here are the things to look out for while texting or calling a person:

1.   Determine how often a person responds to a text message or call. If someone has a job that allows free access to their phone but only responds every five hours, this may indicate a lack of interest. Conversely, if someone is in a job where phone use is prohibited

yet finds ways to respond every few seconds, that may show genuine interest or raise questions.

2. Pay attention to buzzwords used during this phase. For example, does the person frequently use the word "fantastic"? Does the person say "well" a lot? Personality traits are reflected during text message calls. Buzzwords are also a way to connect with the individual's language. Buzzwords also reveal a lot about a person's generation.

3. A person's level of introversion or extraversion depends on their preferred communication method. Introverts usually prefer text messages, while extreme extroverts are open to spontaneous FaceTime calls or frequent calls at any time of day. This can offer insight into who you are dating.

4. Consider what topic of interest fuels the conversation. If someone engages more with flirty sexual messages than with intellectual ones, it suggests potential for a passionate sexual relationship. Conversely, if a person responds to intellectual and financial questions, they are likely a deep thinker. It's essential to understand the personality of the person you're with.

QUESTION
TWENTY-ONE

What is your sex language?

Sex is an essential part of life. Literally, without sex, you wouldn't be reading or listening to this book. Yet, at various points in history, it is something people have held a stigma on discussing until Johnson and Johnson researched the sex cycle.

Sex is a powerful act that releases hormones essential for creating life. Unfortunately, these hormones are often working against us and can cause undesirable effects. Men generally have high levels of testosterone, well, most men. This hormone drives the competitive urge to procreate. Additionally, there are two subtle hormones called oxytocin (the love hormone), which is released in women during orgasms, and vasopressin (the male protective/love hormone), released during orgasms as well. Combined with dopamine (the pleasure hormone that increases the likelihood of repeating behaviors) and serotonin (the feel-good hormone), these chemicals help sex become enjoyable. Finally, after the big orgasm, endorphins (pain relievers and relaxation inducers) help both partners sleep peacefully.

These hormones can be tricky because sex can cause someone to fall in "love" when "love" isn't wanted. It can also lead the wrong people to become obsessive and controlling. For this chapter, imagine you've found someone you're compatible with and are trying to take it to the next level, but before that, you need to know how a person prefers sex, not sex positions—sex.

Over the past decade, love languages and love styles have been popular topics, but I haven't seen anyone talk about the idea of sex languages. So, I'll take a fun step and create something new: the five sex languages. Brace yourself.

A sex language refers to how a person wants to initiate, perform, and conclude sexual activity. In other words, sex language describes how a person chooses to engage in foreplay, play, and end play.

SEX LANGUAGE 1 (THE SEXUAL STRAIGHT SHOOTER)

Straight shooters focus on penetration and orgasm. They usually prefer simple sex positions and want the act over quickly, without foreplay or endplay. They tend to favor sex positions that are straightforward and convenient. Being a straight shooter is also influenced by culture. They are also not gender-specific and tend to be practical individuals who see no reason to wait for a sexual act, for example, in countries where sex is taboo, being a straight shooter is common and doesn't seem perverted or offensive. In societies or religions where men and women are conditioned to avoid pornographic acts or images, anything unusual is avoided. For instance, ejaculating outside of a woman's vagina was considered a waste in ancient Jewish cultures.

Straight shooters are not always boring, but they can be monotonous. For example, it is common for straight shooters to enjoy "quickies" at odd times of the day. Some straight shooters I have met in my practice report that sex is used to quickly alleviate a particular symptom of horniness, stress, anger, or boredom. Once the release is done, it is back to business.

SEX LANGUAGE 2 (THE SEXUAL CROCK POTTER)

Someone with a crockpot sex language likes slow, teasy, sensual sex. There is no hurry or rush, and ejaculation or orgasm are not the primary goals. Crockpotters tend to start the process of sex earlier in the day by flirting, teasing, dropping hints of what's to come, and creating sexual tension. This sexual tension is undeniable, and the release tends to be great.

Crockpotters unconsciously practice sensate focus therapy—an evidence-based technique designed to improve communication and sexual intimacy between partners.

When I suggest sensate focus therapy to my clients, they tend to be a little bit put off by it, and that's because we live in a society that doesn't understand the concept of delayed gratification. In sensate focus therapy, I usually recommend that my clients find a distraction-free environment, get some sensual candles, sensual toys, a dimly lit room, and some good music, and focus on each other's erogenous zones without penetration. The idea is to increase sexual energy until both individuals can't take it anymore. Sensate focus therapy can take place over hours or days of building up sexual intimacy.

Crockpotters have perfected this principle and understand that the journey matters more than the destination.

SEX LANGUAGE 3 (THE SEXUAL PRAGMATIC)

Someone with a pragmatic sex language is specific about what needs to happen for sexual energy to be activated. This may involve experiences that go beyond traditional sexual behaviors in humans. For instance, some individuals become sexually aroused when they receive monetary items, while certain body parts stimulate others. It is not uncommon for the sexually pragmatic to have particular kinks, such as preferences for specific body types, certain clothing items, or a set of precise rituals surrounding sex. A sexual pragmatist might be interested in BDSM, exhibitionism, or other sexual fetishes.

Someone with a sexual pragmatic language may require practicality that sometimes includes scheduled times, specific sex rooms, sex toys, and rituals involving sex. Some with this language are known for consensual non-monogamy, which includes people with similar sexual language. The sexually pragmatic might establish contracts with potential partners because of the nature of their sexual behavior. A popular fictional story, '50 Shades of Grey,' features a character with a sexually pragmatic language, Christian Grey.

SEX LANGUAGE 4 (THE SEXUAL DRAMATIC)

Someone with this sexual language needs intense emotions to enjoy sex. These emotions might be passion or feelings not usually linked to sex. For example, I knew a couple who only had sex after a big argument that made them angry. They said the threat of losing their relationship made sex more exciting because it felt like it could be their last. Some movies also feature intense scenes, such as ripping off clothes, slamming against walls, breaking beds, tearing sheets, and pulling hair, among others. These scenes feature dramatic love acts, multiple positions, and intense emotions.

A woman I worked with told me jealousy made her more daring in bed. After talking, we found she secretly created jealousy to fuel her passion. In such sexual dramas, sex is used to release emotions rather than express them. People who prefer sexual dramas often have a manic love style because chaos fuels their love.

A person with a dramatic sexual language can also have a love language like a sexual Crockpotter, starving their partner of sex as a tease until the crazy lust hormone is released.

SEXUAL LANGUAGE 5 (THE SEXUAL PLEASER)

The sexual pleaser gets pleasure out of pleasuring you. The sexual pleaser is a Master of Art in finding out erogenous zones, precise strokes, licks, etc., that will help a person achieve orgasm. For instance, it is not atypical for the sexual pleaser to perform oral sex on their partner until orgasm, without expecting anything in return. The sexual pleaser can simply orgasm by watching their partner orgasm. The sexual pleaser also knows all the right words to cause a mental orgasm. The sexual pleaser is someone who won't stop having sex until their partner has reached orgasm. The sexual pleaser takes no pleasure in achieving orgasm without their partner achieving orgasm. Sexual pleasers have reported feeling anxious or unwanted when their partners don't achieve orgasm frequently.

Now that you have learned the five sex languages, there is a test below that can help you understand which sex language you have.

The best relationship stage to understand a person's sexual language is the comfort stage. During the awkward stage of a relationship, heightened emotions and neurochemical responses can make a person's sex language confusing because almost anything can turn them on. No one can maintain a false self-language for too long. It's essential to understand your partner's sex language, as this can help determine if you're sexually compatible in the long run.

Although it's recommended to wait until much after the third date before having sex, if you find yourself caught up in the sexual energy cycle, don't worry. Still, ask these questions. Don't make assumptions based solely on initial sexual experiences because people can and often will hide their actual sexual language.

TWENTY-TWO

What are your thoughts on cheating and infidelity?

Most couples avoid this question until it's too late. It has two parts, with one surprising part at the end of this chapter: What would make you cheat, and what do you consider cheating?

According to every available statistic, 69% of divorces result from infidelity and cheating, yet many people don't ask this question within the first three dates. Amazing, right? The more fascinating statistic is the rate of cheating and infidelity between genders. Before the 2000s, it was believed that men engaged in more infidelity than women. However, there is a discrepancy between those who admit to cheating and those who don't.

Statistically, men are more likely to admit to cheating than women. According to Ashley Madison, a website where people can pursue extramarital affairs, women in education and medical fields are more likely to cheat. In contrast, men in trade fields tend to cheat more. Interestingly, the Journal of Sex Research reports that 31% of infidelity occurs in the workplace and is directly linked to income. The Kinsey Institute states that cheating also varies by age; women are more likely to cheat between ages 50 and 69, while men tend to cheat more as they grow older.

Biological and financial principles help explain this. A woman's libido increases as the risk of pregnancy decreases, and testosterone levels tend to rise after menopause. Meanwhile, a man's chances of cheating and infidelity grow with his income. Overall, there seems to be a risk of loss component to infidelity.

As far as reasons behind cheating, Women say that a lack of attention is the main reason they cheat and seek emotional connections while doing so. In contrast, men often engage in multiple one-night stands and tend to be less interested in forming emotional connections.

Despite the statistics, many reasons exist why people cheat, and there are various perspectives on cheating. For example, a study conducted in Europe revealed that a surprising 16% of people do not see intercourse with someone else as cheating because they do not intend to leave their partners.

Overall, the rate of cheating between men and women is equal, but women are less likely to be caught.

Now that we understand how frequently this issue arises in a relationship, let's explore why we should ask this question.

1. **In the talking stage, clearly defining what constitutes cheating is crucial because people have different ideas of what is acceptable during this period.** I've met individuals who believe that until a clear sense of exclusivity is established, "talking" still allows for some degree of freedom to explore.
After the show Bridgerton aired on Netflix, I noticed a shift in ideas about courtship. I explored various African and Indian cultures to see how courtship was conducted and realized it was common for someone to explore multiple options before choosing one. Then I asked, "What then is defined as cheating in the talking stage?" Several dating shows, including Love Is Blind, Love Island, The Bachelor, and The Bachelorette, have emerged, and people seem to subconsciously support the idea that one person can be pursued by many and that the best candidate will ultimately win. However, in real life, people get upset when their partner talks to someone else during the talking phase. That's why you define it. I once met a couple who agreed they are both free agents for any better suitor until marriage. They agreed. It motivated them to

73

make consistent romantic efforts in the relationship and accelerated the marriage.

2. **Asking, "What would make you cheat?" prompts your future partner to reflect on times they may have cheated or been tempted to cheat.** A client of mine once told his wife in my office that if he did not have sex for more than a week, there was a likelihood he would find it elsewhere. This shocked her because he had never communicated this in the beginning. Although his statement was callous, he was honest about his sexual needs, allowing his wife to recognize whether she could manage it or not. Moreover, the conversation would have been more constructive if it had taken place on their second date rather than after years of commitment.

3. **Asking the question will help reduce shock later in life if infidelity or cheating happens.** This doesn't make it right, but previous discussions and boundaries have been set. Jane was an emotionally driven person, married to an emotionless lawyer. She loved love, while he valued practicality. After years of dissatisfaction, Jane ran into an old high school boyfriend at a coffee shop. He was married and going through a divorce. The timing couldn't have been better. After sharing stories of commonalities (ironically, commonalities always exist in relationships because the struggles are universal), they both started a love affair that lasted over two years. Like any love story, even affairs, the honeymoon phase doesn't last forever. They began arguing over the same issues that had led to their initial breakup. He was irresponsible and reckless, traits her husband did not have. Jane quickly realized that her practical husband was what she truly needed, and that passionate, fiery love wasn't always as fulfilling as it seemed. Her boredom in marriage became the reason she chose to stay married and work on her relationship, rather than chasing the excitement of her youth.

At the beginning of this chapter, I said there would be a third part to this question.

Have you ever cheated or been cheated on in a relationship? If so, why did it happen?

A study from the University of Denver revealed striking results to answer this question. People who have cheated in previous relationships are three times more likely to cheat again. Past behavior remains the best predictor of future actions.

No matter which side of the spectrum you are on, you must understand that both you and the other person need to focus on healing before thinking about a relationship. Simply put, the trauma from experiencing either side—being the cheater or the cheated—creates a constant lack of trust in your instincts.

Cheaters are often constantly afraid of being cheated on. At least, most of them are. I usually am not surprised when I see the outrageous reaction of a cheater finally being cheated on.

Most people who have been cheated on are constantly afraid of it happening again. Some rare individuals develop immunity to the feeling and adopt a "break my trust, I walk" principle.

It's important not to judge someone who has cheated in the past, especially if they have acknowledged their mistakes and taken steps to improve. I've seen couples work through their issues and come out stronger after experiencing infidelity from either side. Growth depends on the environment and circumstances. The right person will inspire you to grow and thrive.

TWENTY-THREE

Would you ever consider an open relationship?

Open relationships are becoming increasingly popular. One reason is that some individuals have come to accept that there are many possibilities and exploring them with or without a partner is perfectly acceptable, provided firm boundaries are established. There are seven major types of open relationships.

1. An open marriage/relationship happens when individuals pursue romantic or sexual relationships outside of the marriage.
2. Swinging involves exchanging partners with others for sexual reasons, whether privately or in a group.
3. Increasingly popular, polyamory involves multiple romantic pursuits among consenting adults. There are two types of polyamorous relationships: hierarchical polyamory and non-hierarchical polyamory. In hierarchical polyamory, a primary relationship is prioritized while other romantic partners are pursued. In non-hierarchical polyamory, there is no prioritized relationship.
4. Monogamish involves one primary relationship along with occasional casual sex with others.
5. Hybrid relationships occur when one partner is monogamous, and the other is not.

6. Quad relationships involve four people who share some romantic or sexual connections, though not necessarily with each other.
7. Triad relationships involve three people who have a romantic relationship with each other.

In my younger years, a man approached me at a nightclub. He grinned and pointed at his wife on the dance floor. I smiled back with a similar grin. He said, "You know she likes you…that's my wife. You can come by tonight." I did a double-take at his gorgeous wife and ran the other way. That was the first time I ever experienced such a thing. He was serious, and she was serious. I was flattered, but the couple's power and confidence felt suspicious. I instantly imagined being tied to a basement pole, crying for help. It was too good to be true. I mean, "How can you let your beautiful wife sleep with another man?"

Three years later, I came to understand that they were practicing consensual non-monogamy. It worked for them and others. Every relationship is different. Asking this question creates an open space to discuss opening the relationship before thoughts of infidelity creep in. It also allows you to understand what you can handle.

As a therapist experienced in supporting multiple open relationships, I recognize that these arrangements often involve discomfort and uncertainty until everyone feels secure and comfortable. When there is anxious attachment in any open relationship, it can cause jealous and irrational behaviors that may trigger deep wounds of abandonment, neglect, guilt, and mistrust.

Someone who cannot communicate should not be in an open relationship. Openness requires vulnerability and understanding. It is impossible to avoid anxiety if secrecy becomes the norm. Open relationships must follow strict rules. Straying from these rules can lead to severe mistrust and the same physiological response as if one has been cheated on.

Frank and Janine had been married for ten years when they decided to open their relationship. They decided to be monogamish and then transitioned into an open marriage. Frankie and Janine set strict rules, which boiled down to, "We come first, always." Frank had a girlfriend, and Janine had a boyfriend. It was perfect. Janine had a boyfriend who loved shopping with her, and Frank had a girlfriend who was interested in skydiving. The two ensured they were a priority until Janine's boyfriend began creating retirement plans and drunkenly told someone that he would swoop Janine and move to South America. This news leaked to Frank. Unpleased about this, Frank demanded an explanation. Janine told Frank she would break up with her boyfriend after days of debating.

Now, you may be thinking, "This is awesome." But no, Frank was left with the guilt of watching his wife go through a breakup, and soon Janine demanded that Frank break up with his girlfriend. This led to a rift between them, and they ended up in my office to discuss the matter.

In all fairness, Frank found out that Janine considered the idea of moving to South America with another man, while Frank never made any comments or tried to leave. Janine said that if she weren't in a relationship with someone else, Frank wouldn't have the right to be in a relationship with his girlfriend. Frank didn't hesitate to tell us that he was willing to prioritize breaking up with his girlfriend over his marriage, but he felt an unsettling sense of unfairness.

When I asked if all these issues had been discussed before opening the relationship, both admitted they had not discussed what would constitute a break-up.

In open relationships, it is typical for situations like these to happen eventually. Someone usually gets hurt unless all parties have a mutual understanding. Frank never met with Janine's boyfriend to discuss the rules, and neither did Janine meet with Frank's girlfriend. Frank and Janine were on the same page, but the boyfriend and girlfriend were not, which hurt them.

1. The number one rule of an open relationship is "do no harm, " including primary and secondary parties.
2. The rules of an open relationship should always be tailored to each person and agreed upon by everyone involved before the establishment of the relationship.
3. Understand that breaking the rules of an open relationship is considered cheating. For instance, if specific individuals or

locations are off-limits, breaking the rules, regardless of the relationship being open, constitutes cheating.

4. More effort must be invested in the primary relationship than the secondary one for it to succeed, unless everyone agrees to maintain equality.

5. When you ask this question, remember that even if someone agrees to consider an open relationship, they still have the right to say no later.

QUESTION

TWENTY-FOUR

——⋆⟨◈⟩⋆——

What are your goals?

In my first book, Relationship Code, I describe a gentleman deeply involved in politics and a woman who craved solitude and privacy. They experience what is known as the 'right person, wrong situation.' Everything seemed perfect for them; they shared many interests and met all the questions and criteria outlined in this book. The main issue was that Jason intended to run for mayor, which would thrust their family matters into the public eye. Stacy wanted no part of this. Fortunately, before they got engaged, they ended their relationship. Months later, Jason met another extroverted woman eager to support his political ambitions.

For a successful marriage, the goals of you and your partner must align. No amount of emotional affection or love will sustain a future marriage with opposing goals. Jen, a middle-aged woman, loves everything about medical school. She played with medical toys from a young age and dreamed of becoming a surgeon. Jen was a straight-A student who excelled in her science classes. After graduating from college, she met a man at work. Peter was a big teddy bear whom she loved dearly. Jen cherished this about him during the first two years of medical school, as they spent a lot of time together. However, when Jen began discussing what medical school would involve over the next seven years, Peter started to withdraw, realizing there would be little chance for marriage, homeownership, or children while pursuing her medical career. He was profoundly hurt and understood that she would hardly have time for him once her residency began. Faced with this reality, she had to choose between her passion and her career. Their life goals were not aligned, and she soon seemed to be considering dropping out of medical school to fulfill the dreams and ideals Peter had for his life. Peter completed law school, and his career flourished while Jen worked in a biology lab. Over time, resentment grew, and divorce became inevitable. Jen sacrificed her ambitions for the family she hoped to create, only to regret it. Once the divorce occurred, Jen returned to medical school and fulfilled her lifelong dream of becoming a surgeon. Due to the demands of her surgeon lifestyle, where she was constantly on call, she recognized the need for a partner who could primarily manage things at home. Like another story in this book, Jen began dating someone who traded on the stock market from home and was willing to stay home with the children.

Your goals must align. The problem I've observed with many couples is that they believe that mismatched goals will solve themselves eventually. This mindset often lacks honesty about true desires and can lead to resentment. Always conduct a reality check when examining a potential future relationship. If you realize you are a police officer but your partner dislikes the anxiety that comes with that lifestyle, don't marry someone who cannot handle being with a police officer. High divorce rates result from couples entering relationships without sufficient thought, forgetting that logic is essential in relationships.

If you're struggling to understand your life goals, that's OK. Focus on the present. However, this question cannot be addressed if an individual does not know themselves and has not identified their life's purpose. These are things you need to understand before forming a relationship. Another essential consideration is everything else in this book. For instance, if you are with someone who has an anxious attachment style, you know that you need to be around this person as often as possible to help ease anxiety or provide reassurance of wanting to be in the relationship. Now, if you're in a job requiring you to travel halfway across the world, that would not be a good idea. Again, the questions in this book will help you reflect on your goals.

TWENTY-FIVE

How can I help you achieve your goals?

The practicality of relationships needs more discussion today. We must start viewing relationships as two business partnerships, both built on the foundation of love. You can't achieve certain things if your partner is working against you. It won't be easy. One thing I notice people overlook at the start of a relationship is how they can support each other's careers. There seems to be an individualistic mindset regarding the relationship's goals.

Ask your partner how they think you can help with their goals. This gives you an idea of what you can do to assist or what you can offer. For example, in the previous chapter, I discussed a doctor's experience in medical school. If her partner asked how he could help, she would probably say, "Hey, there's going to be a time in our lives when I cannot be available anymore, and during that timeframe, I would like us to work together to figure out ways to raise our family while not neglecting our careers." He would respond positively, saying, "Maybe I can sacrifice two or three days a week to stay home with the kids all day, or perhaps we should find a babysitter." The key here is addressing potential problems before they occur.

Jake wanted to start his business as a State Farm Insurance broker. I know the irony of using the word Jake, but I promise it's not Jake from the State Farm commercial. To become a private insurance broker, Jake knew he had to quit his well-paying job and risk not having enough clients for his new business. Aware of this from the start while dating, he did not hesitate to tell his potential partners what he needed from them for this endeavor. Of course, Jake being a man posed a disadvantage because most women don't want to hear that there's a possibility of financial insecurity in the future. This was before he met Sarah. Sarah was a realtor, and before Jacob could finish his sentence, Sarah said, "You know what? I can help you with your business by making sure everyone in my realtor business knows about the insurance product you offer." This brought so much joy to Jake that he did not hesitate to propose to her six months later. The two's businesses and passions complemented each other and thrived.

Another inspiring story comes from someone who has a disability. She was in a car accident at 18 and lost the use of her legs. All she wanted in life was a complete family with children. She understood she would need a partner to fill the gaps in her knowledge. Her future husband, a man with a big heart, acted on her wishes to help her achieve her goals. Although he was busy with the construction business, he assured her he would make time for her and the children no matter what.

I work with couples for premarital counseling. I have them list their goals for one, two, three, five, and ten years to help them see ways they can assist each other in accomplishing their goals. ***You need to understand your partner's destination to understand if the journey would be tolerable.***

Another aspect of this exercise is writing down strengths. For instance, I have seen situations where one person in the relationship is more skilled at managing finances than the other, or one person excels at managing multiple jobs. I have also observed instances where one person is more adept at household tasks than another. I believe every couple should handle their partnership based on the strength-based approach. It makes life easier and simpler. The point of the questions in this book is to discover your future partner's strengths, weaknesses, ways to complement both, and most importantly, the decision to be part of the journey. Couples often argue over petty issues because they do not employ a strength-based approach.

The strength-based approach helps keep couples strong and resilient. For example, a client mentioned he hates doing laundry but enjoys folding and putting it away. This works well for his partner because she likes doing laundry but dislikes folding and putting it away. Without this understanding, before entering a relationship or marriage, they might have argued constantly over laundry.

QUESTION
TWENTY-SIX

❖

A condo or a house?

Initially, I removed this question from the book. However, I decided to include it again as a rhetorical inquiry to identify where your future partner would like to live. Asking about a house or a condo is a preliminary question to determine the type of neighborhood or location that your future partner prefers. I have encountered people who dislike the idea of a house with a white picket fence. Conversely, I have also met men and women who would not appreciate high-rise apartments with a concierge. Different people have different needs. Inquiring about a house or condo also serves as a way to gauge one's financial commitment. Some individuals are comfortable renting for their entire lives, allowing for easy mobility, while others aspire to be homeowners.

Again, it's all about ensuring you are on the same page. Stacy and Abraham met in an apartment complex. They glanced at each other in the elevator and smiled until Stacy mustered the courage to invite Abraham to her apartment to finish the Chinese takeout she had gotten. The two hit it off quickly, and soon, they were ready to say " I do. " Stacy promptly requested a house with a big backyard for the kids to play. Abraham was accustomed to having people valet his car, not worrying about lawn mowing, and paying high HOA fees to avoid the stresses of house upkeep. Naturally, Abraham embraced the adage that a happy wife means a happy life and decided to buy a house for Stacy. However, the couple found themselves bickering over outdoor chores. Abraham had allergies that prevented him from cutting grass, and Stacy disliked the idea of a woman mowing the lawn. They resolved the issue by hiring landscaping experts, leading to thousands of dollars spent on lawn care every summer. Additionally, Abraham disliked snow because he didn't have to deal with it in his comfortable condo, which had a garage and valet service.

Neighborhoods also matter. As Stacy grew, she preferred a larger house with more land, which meant they had to move farther from the city. Abraham complied with his wife's request. However, it wasn't long before Abraham resented this and soon became distant due to his frequent trips to the city. Abraham's lifestyle was city-based, whereas Stacy was accustomed to living in the country, where she had grown up. Despite their emotional connection, lifestyle differences ultimately led to the couple's separation.

Know your future partner.

What are your social media expectations?

In some ancient civilizations, there were Town Criers. The Town Crier's job was to make public announcements in local squares where people gathered, allowing news to spread quickly through word of mouth. The Town Crier would announce if someone was getting married, having children, or if a war was impending. This was a semi-efficient way of disseminating information for those who heard it directly from the Town Crier; however, others would likely receive distorted information from a second party. Think of the game "Telephone. "

In this century, we no longer have Town Criers, but Town Criers are now featured in the media as popular news outlets, such as TMZ, The Shade Room, and CNN. These platforms maintain an adequate social media presence on Facebook, Snapchat, TikTok, Instagram, and other platforms. Whether we like it or not, these platforms have created a compelling form that allows us to be Town Criers, spin truths, and over-objectify personal opinion.

Introspectively speaking, there is always a primary news event, such as a tornado destroying a town. This primary news event is reported by a primary news source, which includes major news networks and newspapers. The primary news source leads to secondary news sources, which include micro news outlets and individual journalists. At each level, a version of the truth is distorted, often based on political, religious, or personal biases. For instance, CNN might discuss the tornado, MSNBC may address the right wing's lack of involvement in aid efforts, and FOX News could focus on the left wing's involvement in efforts as the information trickles down. Some public members will begin to form their own beliefs and opinions before sharing them with even more micro levels.

When it comes to individuals, some of us post pictures whenever we visit our favorite restaurant or vacation spot, while others observe quietly in ghost mode to gather information. With each picture posted, people form opinions based on your photo. Some may see that you're happy and want to be like you, while others may see that you're sad and feel sorry for you. The viewer's interpretation of your photo conveys information that cannot be controlled. Social media allows interpretations to run wild, which is why an individual's level of privacy on social media also correlates with their personality type. Extroverts tend to post more, whereas introverts typically post less.

Carla had one million followers on Instagram and made it a point to post daily. She would wake up for work, dress in a professional outfit, and take multiple photos from different angles before heading to work. Despite having multiple endorsements from shoe and clothing brands, she continued her job as a Nurse Practitioner.

Tim, a local accountant, was the opposite. He loved being discreet and was satisfied with his twenty-five followers. He posted one picture on Instagram that barely showed his face, and he always kept his account private.

When I met them, I knew there would be a problem. Carla had multiple male trolls on her page, and Tim, though secure in his position in Carla's life, did not like the sexual attention she was drawing from these men. Despite this, he never discouraged Carla from posting pictures and even took some of her most liked pictures for her.

When the two became more serious, Carla took a photo of them to post on her social media account, and Tim said no outright. Carla, offended, took it as Tim being shifty about his commitment to her and possibly being ashamed of her.

Before I go further, please note that posting relationships on social media is not abnormal behavior. Humans have done it for centuries to mark their territory. It is just that the way we do it is much more intrusive because it leaves room for people to dig into your partner's whole life by clicking on a tag.

Engaging in discussions about social media expectations is essential in today's world. Here are the questions you can ask.

- What do you think about changing your relationship status on Facebook?
- Do you post on social media often?
- What social media apps do you use primarily?
- What types of people follow your social media account?
- How would it appear if we posted all the time and then suddenly stopped, deleting all our photos?
- Are you comfortable with our future kids being posted publicly?
- What is your privacy battery status?
- Are you comfortable with exes being unblocked or blocked? What about the ex-partner's family and friends?
- If our families follow each other, are there any rules about posting based on your family's expectations? For example, what would your family say if I posted a bikini photo or a post expressing strong political beliefs?

Many follow-up questions can be added to this, which may already have answers based on your future partner's current social media privacy settings.

What a person posts and what they do not post can reveal a great deal about them. Pay attention. For instance, a person posting everything except their partner may indicate a red or green flag. If a person only posts their partner, it may suggest a red or green flag. If a person shares too much, it may be a red flag. It may also be a red flag if someone does not post. Every individual is different. The reasons for each answer will provide insight into what you are or are not comfortable with.

Carla and Tim had to learn to be cautious. Carla explained she needed reassurance because posting about their relationship helped her show off her man and keep unwanted attention from other men at bay. Tim agreed to occasional posts, but this created bigger problems. Social media can be a toxic space. When a woman is desired and envied by many men, and she finally shares a picture of her man, there's often a need for scrutiny and unfair judgment. Tim had to read comments like "I expected more," and "Come be with a real man." He had to learn to handle negative opinions in the name of love.

Not everyone's experience is like Carla and Tim's. Sasha and James met in high school and were captivated by one another. James aspired to become a police officer and spent considerable time figuring out the best way to enter law enforcement. After earning his bachelor's degree in criminal justice, he applied for several positions until he secured a better opportunity to work on a Federal Government task force. Sasha had some friends from high school who followed her on all social media platforms and were "not so good." They used drugs, partied hard, and engaged in many other illegal activities that shouldn't have been posted online. Sasha attended several parties in college, and although she didn't participate in any illegal activities, she could be seen in the background of various photos.

During James's background check, these photos were discovered online, which made James a less-than-ideal candidate for this task force.

Remember, the internet retains all information. Who you associate with and how they post matters significantly.

The final example in this chapter features a man named Jake. Jake is a serial monogamist who was never bitter enough to block his ex-girlfriends on social media. All his exes followed him and would occasionally like or comment on his posts. Jake maintained good boundaries and refrained from making friendly comments that crossed the line. However, this didn't sit well with the woman trying to date Jake. Emily believed that doors needed to be closed and locked, and that the keys should be thrown away to avoid temptation. Although Jake frequently posted pictures with Emily and included clear captions to show his love for her, Emily felt insecure because he had done the same for every woman he had been with in the past.

After months of disagreement, Emily told Jake she wanted him to permanently delete and block his exes and their families on his Facebook and Instagram accounts. Jake was caught off guard because none of his exes had ever asked him to do something so intimate. He argued that they could all testify he had never cheated, but she insisted. Jake deleted and blocked everyone to prove his loyalty to Emily, but he resented her for not feeling "secure" with him enough. Emily didn't realize that Snapchat had never been a focus because she couldn't see who followed him there. One day, she found a message thread on Snapchat where Jake explained to an ex why he had to block her, which started a cycle of mistrust and insecurity in the relationship.

Here are the facts: More couples are breaking up over social media issues than ever before. Most cheaters tend to meet their affair partners online. Social media has increasingly become a space where distrust can grow. Ensure that you discuss boundaries and expectations.

TWENTY-EIGHT

How many children do you want?

This question is significant in learning what your partner can handle financially, emotionally, and physically. For instance, if a woman is in her late thirties or forties, a man coming in with the expectation of having four children is medically risky. Many couples also discuss how many children they want without considering the cost.

For instance, if you and your potential partner have an income cap/limit based on your chosen profession, ensuring that the number of children you want is affordable is crucial, given that your income does not change. Ensure your future partner is also aware of the commitments needed to raise the desired number of children.

My father always told me, "Never sleep with anyone you would not consider being the mother of your child." And though I have neglected that rule several times, I possess a keen understanding that any sexual relationship could lead to long-term parenting with someone you hate. Because of this awareness, I encourage my clients to thoroughly assess whoever they share their bed with to avoid future complications.

Jacob and Trisha fell in love within the first few minutes of meeting. They asked many of the questions in this book and seemed to agree on everything except one point. Jacob wanted a maximum of one child, and possibly two if the first child was bored and needed a sibling to play with. Trisha grew up in a family of nine and loved the noise and chaos of multiple people living under one roof. Out of her love for Jacob, she compromised on having three children instead of the six she desired. After their first child, Jacob developed cold feet due to the stress of being a new parent, and he reluctantly agreed to have a second child. When the pressure to have a third child became more intense, Jacob booked a trip to Vegas with his guy friends but never actually went. There was no trip. Instead, he visited the urologist, underwent a vasectomy, and stayed on his best friend's couch for seven days to recover.

For months, his wife had no clue there was no trip, and Trisha found it unusual that suddenly, Jacob had no anxiety about "pulling out." Her instincts kicked in, and the timing of tax season validated her suspicions. Every year, she handled the household taxes due to her background in accounting. This particular year, she realized Jacob had a lot of extra money. She noted no transactions in Las Vegas when sifting through his bank statements. Suspicious that he was cheating, she stormed at him with many questions. When confronted, he realized he had a choice: pretend he cheated or confess to an even worse deception—one that was guaranteed to end his marriage.

This level of deception isn't abnormal. I have heard several stories where men choose to get a vasectomy against the will of their partner. Still, Jacob's situation was particularly unique because he kept a secret for over a year without giving his wife a choice. After weeks of questioning Jacob's half-truths, he finally confessed. Trisha used these words: "It would have been easier for me to forgive a cheating partner than a man who watched me question my fertility and played in my face." Jacob's response was, "I knew I would lose her for sure if I did not have a third child, and I knew I would lose myself if I had a third child. I chose myself."

This discussion is critical. Everyone has a preference, and not everyone is willing to compromise. No matter how much you love someone, children are a critical topic of discussion due to the physical, financial, and emotional costs associated with them.

TWENTY-NINE

What is your parenting style?

This might be a weird third-date question, but it is essential. Thanks to social media platforms, discussions on parental trauma are becoming more mainstream. At the beginning of this book, I reiterated that as a Doctor of Psychology who has spent years studying trauma and various forms of mental illnesses, I have realized that the most critical institution today is the family, which stems from relationships.

Who you choose to sleep with is so vital that it can alter multiple historical outcomes. If people understood the importance of the mating game, many physical and mental illnesses would be avoided or prepared for; many things we consider generational curses would also be prevented. Relationships can be the breeding ground for creating a psychopath or an empath, a batterer or a nurturer, a grower or a destroyer.

It is shocking to me to see how much people take this for granted. A person's parenting style is directly correlated with how much trauma may be passed on to the next generation.

- Authoritative parents tend to give their children the flexibility to grow by creating open lines of communication, setting rules, and solving problems together.
- Authoritarian parents have high levels of discipline and control, low levels of warmth, and one-way communication, with little to no consideration of what the child needs.

- Permissive parents tend to have low expectations, are highly responsive, rarely enforce rules, and overindulge the child.
- Neglectful/uninvolved parents tend to fulfill their children's basic needs but are emotionally detached or disengaged.

Mainstream culture has tagged other types of parents as helicopter parents (micro-managers), narcissistic parents (selfish and absorbed), etc. If you pay attention to the details of parenting styles, you can make predictions about what your child will be like with your parenting style. You can also identify what can induce trauma and harm children.

Although other outcomes can predict a child's future, parenting style can influence whether a parent is even aware of those outcomes. A simple example is how to breed a sociopath or psychopath. It's easy: avoid providing your child with any form of emotional warmth during the first five years of existence, expose them to severe trauma and violence, and give them no moral code to go by. Boom. There you go! Sociopath.

Most of life involves social learning, which primary caregivers facilitate. If you aim to raise responsible and kind humans, ensure you choose a responsible and kind partner.

A client once said, "Well, I know he is an absent father, but I can compensate for the absence if we are married. My question was, what if you divorced?" When thinking about a future partner, ask, "Do I trust this person to care for my offspring if I am not present?" If the answer is no, don't entertain a second date, hoping they can change. Specific lessons are learned naturally, while others are learned through force. I met a gentleman who was so consumed by the beauty of his woman that he forgot to consider her lifestyle. She was a wild-spirited woman whose weekends always involved as many parties as possible. I was surprised when he was surprised about her increased symptoms of depression while pregnant and her decision to hop back into nightlife once the baby was out of her stomach. To make matters worse, he felt a better solution was to divorce and split custody. This was one of the rawest counseling sessions I've had with anyone. I asked him why he would trust her to watch his child alone, given that he knew who she was. Of course, he took a chance and soon realized his baby went to these "parties" with his mother, exposed to drugs, booze, and sex.

There are telltale signs that indicate what a person would be like as a parent.

1. Are they patient and kind with children? Don't expect a person who isn't kind to other children to be kind to their own.
2. Are children receptive to them? Children are highly attuned to energy. You can pretend, but energy doesn't lie, and some children pick up on that energy.
3. Did they have good parents as role models? Social learning is essential. A person's parents' parenting style can influence their parenting approach. Knowing what your partner's parents are like romantically can also predict how they will behave with you. This is easier to observe when you have the chance to meet the parents or caregivers. Breaking familiar habits is difficult unless one is aware and is making an effort to do better.
4. Is this person kind to elders or individuals with disabilities? Their approach to caring for elders or those who cannot care for themselves reveals much about their character.
5. Does this person have a good stress tolerance? A person's ability to remain calm and level-headed in highly stressful situations is crucial to understanding what it would be like to be a parent.
6. Is this person good with money? Most people forget that financial management is a key quality of a good parent. Making the most of little is a genuine skill that many people lack. This aspect is especially crucial in marriage.
7. Does this person possess the necessary skills to raise another human alone? Don't focus solely on what can be done in your presence. The divorce rate is 50%, so you must consider what can be accomplished in your absence.

As a child custody evaluator, I am concerned that many people do not consider this chapter until divorce court, when the question of custody time arises. We live in a new world and must pay attention to it.

THIRTY

If we were to divorce, what would the custody arrangement look like?

I know nobody gets married to get divorced, but we need to understand that one out of every two married people, or 50% of marriages, end in divorce. As a divorce counselor, I have worked with several couples and families to try to repair the damage caused by divorce. One thing I understand is that there is almost always bitterness when divorce happens. The person who loves you, with songs, kisses, and the words, "I would never hurt you," will hurt you if you file for divorce against them. It's the harsh truth. It is very rare to see the absence of bitterness in a divorce.

Many times, women tend to be the ones guilty of parental alienation, AND in my experience, it is not just about punishment, it is about survival. Parental alienation syndrome consists of a series of symptoms caused by one parent deciding to keep the other parent away from the children for unjust reasons. This is sometimes a malicious attempt to retaliate against the other parent for choosing to end the commitment. Sadly, I have observed both genders engage in this behavior; however, women are often more guilty of parental alienation. This issue is so pervasive in the court system that it has established child custody evaluation guidelines for psychologists, therapists, and social workers to determine who will receive the most parenting time.

Unfortunately, as a clinician, I take no pride or joy in granting one parent custody over the other, especially knowing that both parents can be good if they set their pride aside for the child's sake. I always find it disturbing that the parent keeping the child away from the other parent does not realize that this separation benefits no one and ultimately harms the child more. That said, I firmly believe, much like any prenuptial agreement, there should be an agreement on what custody will entail in the event of a divorce. Again, I'm not suggesting you ask this question to gauge what the other parent would do, as they would likely be uncertain until that situation arises. However, consider this: no matter how strong, love diminishes when mistakes are made in marriages and relationships. One reason this question is among the last in this book is that if you ask your future partner all the other questions, you can gain insight into what might happen if you divorce. I urge everyone to reflect on what their partner's parents were like during their childhood. I emphasize this because I've noticed a pattern: a woman whose mother exhibited parental alienation in her upbringing tends to repeat the same patterns, based on my observations in clinical practice. One of my clients even remarked that it is the mother's prerogative to choose who can see her children. I had to correct her firmly by stating that both parents have rights.

We live in a feminist era where men and women can raise children. Now, this question is entirely different if one person says, "Hey, I know I cannot take responsibility due to my conditions." That's OK, but to get to a space where you're fighting and keeping the kids away from the other willing, healthy parents because of bitterness or hurt, causes nothing but pain for the children. I was counseling one child one day, and she told me she didn't understand why her parents were still fighting. In her words, "They might as well just beat together". I asked this little girl why, and she said, "If you are still fighting after separation, then you might as well be together and miserable". This little girl's statement had me thinking for days because I often wonder why children tend to say less during custody battles.

If you take the questions in this book seriously, you will avoid ending up in a custody battle. For instance, if you already know that your partner has an alcohol use disorder, you will be aware of what the custody battle will look like because she won't want your kids to stay overnight with someone irresponsible with alcohol. This question can save many heartaches for partners, children, and future generations.

Jamison reluctantly agreed to be the household's sole breadwinner. As a result, Jamison worked endless hours, and with those hours came increasing exposure to his new secretary. Soon, he succumbed to temptation and began having an affair with her. When his wife, Clara, discovered this, she filed for divorce immediately. Scared, Jamison pleaded with her, saying, "Kids are involved in this, and we can handle it." He wanted 50-50 custody but found himself in a difficult position, as courts typically favor the parent who spends the most time with the children.

Although Jamison had always been a responsible father before agreeing to be the family's sole breadwinner, Clara reinforced the narrative that he should not have custody. This situation devastated him when the court granted his wife majority custody, allowing him access to his children for only six days a month, during which Clara discouraged any time spent together. After two and a half years of relentless custody battles, Clara managed to heal from the infidelity, but the damage was done. Jamison lost all possible relationships with his children and had to work three times harder to get them into the car with him. He was deeply hurt. For readers, you might say Jamison deserves this fate, or perhaps he doesn't, but one thing remains clear: the kids did not deserve to be without a father due to their mother's inability to let go of her pain for their sake. In my assessment, Jamison was a good father who struggled to adapt to his new role as a single parent, especially as his separation from his wife had halved his expenses. I believe he sacrificed for his family and deserved to see his children. It's difficult for me to cite examples of parental alienation since I rarely see men do it. However, one unique case involved a man who used parental alienation as revenge against his ex-wife for keeping the kids away from him for so long. I often advise parents that the only people they hurt are their children. Kids deserve to see both parents, and if one parent is unhealthy, it is my job as a child custody evaluator to recommend the best course of action to get the parents back to a stable baseline.

THIRTY-ONE

What are your thoughts on signing a prenuptial agreement?

In my earliest dating experience, I always emphasized to the women I was dating that a prenup had to be signed, and I was surprised that many women took offense to it. Again, no one gets married to get divorced, so a prenup needs to be signed to get married, which sounds weird. However, divorce is as common as sunrise and sunset, and many people enter relationships for the wrong reasons. A recent statistic revealed that most women's wealth originated from assets acquired during a divorce. Now that women are earning more, the influx of irresponsible men marrying with the potential to gain something after a divorce has also increased. A couple should have the right to discuss signing a prenuptial agreement together; if both agree that a prenuptial agreement is unnecessary, it does not have to be signed.

The main issue arises when one person wants a prenup and the other doesn't, leading many of my clients to ask me, "Should I still go ahead with a marriage?" My answer is always no. If you're not comfortable with something, don't do it. No matter how much you love someone, if you need to sign a prenup to protect the assets you've earned through hard work, do it sooner rather than later. I stress this because, as a marriage counselor, I see how quickly couples can shift from deep love to deep resentment. It doesn't take much for hostility to develop. I could give many examples of disturbing situations, but we've all seen plenty on television shows featuring reality stars, politicians, and entertainers.

Gem collectors who marry often do so for financial reasons. A prenup doesn't necessarily indicate that you will not receive anything in the event of a divorce; it simply means that the terms agreed upon before the marriage should be honored.

In 2014, I had one of the best jobs I've ever had. It made me take becoming a therapist more seriously. I was an Uber driver, and as sad as that sounds, I loved it. I cherished every moment because I got to talk to many people from different walks of life about a wide range of topics. One day, I picked up a lawyer who chose to sit in the passenger seat instead of the back. The trip lasted 20 minutes, and I was able to ask her about the pros and cons of her job. She said she loved the pay but hated the bitterness and anger it involved. She looked at me and said, "If you know what's good for you, you should ensure you agree on things before marriage." I asked her why, and she told me that trusting your future husband or wife is like believing the brand-new car you bought will run forever. Her statement was true. There is a thin line between love and hate, and I have seen it in several post-divorce and even marriage counseling sessions.

Some individuals are so committed to hurting their partners after divorce that they forget that inflicting pain on others will not alleviate their suffering. I worked with a woman during my first years in private practice. She was going through a divorce from a wealthy man and received $300,000 for the house, cars, the dogs, primary custody of the kids, and a monthly alimony payment. Her ex-husband accidentally told somebody, " I don't care how much money she takes from me; I would hate if she took the precious tools that my father gave me. " To my greatest surprise, she included those tools as part of her demands for the divorce.

People can be very spiteful when upset, which is one of the reasons why you shouldn't be in a relationship with somebody capable of such behavior. When the push comes to shove, everyone is looking out for their own best interest. In this situation, she did not need the tools. She did not need the $300,000. She did not need the house. She was already getting a monthly alimony check of $10,000.

Another gentleman I worked with years ago married a beautiful doctor. When he met her, he had a job. After three years of dating, they eventually married. He quit his job, stayed home, and tried to run several failed businesses. Having a wife who made $500,000 a year was great, but because of his lack of responsibility towards any job, he started cheating. When she found out, she decided to file for divorce after multiple attempts to forgive him. When the court case arrived, he took advantage of the situation and walked away from that marriage with over $1 million in alimony checks.

Paying attention to people's family history is crucial. Typically, parents who are spiteful during a divorce often have children who become spiteful themselves in their divorces. It is a learned behavior. The apple does not fall far from the tree. Divorce attorneys often advise that it's unwise not to sign a prenup, whether you expect to stay married for life or anticipate a divorce someday. Remember, a prenup doesn't mean you're not giving your partner anything; it simply outlines what you agree to give and what you won't. A marriage is a contract, whether we like it or not. If you haven't signed a prenuptial agreement, don't worry—you can sign a postnuptial agreement.

CHAPTER

THIRTY-TWO

What are your thoughts on spirituality?

In my lifetime, I have rarely met couples with opposing religions, faiths, or spiritualities who manage to sustain a long-term relationship. I do see couples without faith, religion, or spirituality who are successful. There are exceptions, and those depend on several factors. I come from a family of Muslims and Christians, so it is common for people within my family to date or marry across both religions. There is deep respect for Islamic and Christian traditions like Ramadan, Christmas, and Easter. This respect comes from a genuine understanding and familiarity with both. The key word is "familiarity," which most couples with opposing faiths rarely take the time to develop.

Another factor to consider is the strength of a person's faith or spirituality. If faith and spirituality play a significant role in your life, be sure to mention it during the first three dates, as you may spend the rest of your life with this person. Additionally, you want to see if your lifestyle aligns with their spirituality and vice versa.

I once met a woman who practiced good witchcraft. Her spirituality was nature-based, heavily centered on tarot card readings and other rituals I didn't understand. Although we were financially, intellectually, physically, and socially compatible, I knew she mocked the idea that I attended church and was resistant to what Christianity calls evil. Through my dating experience with her, I learned the difference between spirituality and religion. Spirituality creates and maintains a direct connection with your higher power, whereas religion is organized spirituality centered on a source and a set of rules. It wasn't long before I realized that no matter how many feelings I had, our spirits couldn't align because of our different beliefs.

I once had a couple come into my office. The man was an atheist, while she was a strong Christian. At that time, they had been married for five years. Neither had an issue with their spirituality or lack thereof until they began having children, which led to debates about exposing them to the Christian religion that started to tear them apart. He was resistant to what he called "indoctrination" schools. He believed his children should grow up with knowledge of all religions and form their own opinions when they reached enlightenment. She believed the only way to raise morally decent children was to take them to a morally decent institution—the church.

Indeed, a happy wife and a happy life are recurring themes in many potentially resentful marriages. As a result, she got her way, while he bit his tongue each time he picked up the kids from Christian school.

Personally and professionally, I have found that it is best to be with someone who shares your spiritual values. You don't need to share the same beliefs; however, it is essential to align with your partner's beliefs, which means supporting them in their faith and spirituality. If you consider their faith or spirituality as absolute garbage, don't stress; move on to the next relationship.

THIRTY-THREE

What is your legal history?

By the time you reach this chapter, you will know the answer to this question. A client of mine dubbed herself the "felon honey"—as a joke, of course. She couldn't understand why she always seemed to attract men with extensive legal histories. From the horror stories I have heard, I learned to add this to my list of questions. Legal history doesn't have to be extreme. It can be a minor crime. For example, some individuals are notorious for receiving speeding tickets. If you know this about your future partner, consider your safety while they drive.

In contrast, others have navigated multiple divorces. A common mistake most people make is to assume that a divorcee has been divorced only once. A client of mine knew his wife had been divorced when they met, but later discovered she was on her sixth marriage. We dubbed her the Nomadic Spouse (a traveler who marries, divorces, and then relocates to a different state or country), which will be discussed in my next book. This type of individual goes beyond a gem collector; they are diamond gem collectors.

Extreme examples to watch for include sex offenders; these predators target vulnerable men and women, particularly those with children. Felicia was a no-nonsense woman whom most people feared. She was so intimidating that most people avoided her. Felicia described herself as an angry woman and enjoyed how her employees and children fell in line when she arrived. One day, that changed when she met the most patient man she had ever known, Christopher. Christopher cared for her children as if they were his own, and it wasn't long before Felicia began noticing strange behaviors. For the sake of not triggering anyone reading this, it was discovered that he was a sex offender. I have often recommended that some of my clients get background checks before introducing a potential partner to their children.

Another overlooked crime is financial fraud. Jeremy identified himself as a social media influencer and internet sales entrepreneur. Laura loved his independence, his lavish spending on dates and travel, and that he traveled whenever he wanted. Two months into their relationship, the gifts stopped, and this time around, he began asking her for money with promises of repaying her once his internet fortunes were restored. She believed him and was shelling out thousands of dollars to him. She didn't mind. After all, he spent a lot on Gucci, Prada, and other name-brand products for her. Six months of paying him over $20,000 led Laura to search his browser for his entrepreneurial activity. To her astonishment, she discovered that not only was Jeremy a fraud, but he was also a cheater who had many "hard-working" girlfriends who funded his habits. People like Jeremy are common. They are so common that Netflix has begun profiting from documentaries relating to fraudulent spouses who take advantage of innocent women and men.

If you come across someone with a history of financial fraud, be cautious about sharing your Social Security number and financial information. I'm sure you understand my point. Some individuals rehabilitate after a serious offense, while others do not and become increasingly adept at committing more severe offenses.

This concludes my book. I hope you enjoyed reading it as much as I enjoyed gathering and writing down the information. Remember, your time should not be wasted on the dating game. Don't compromise on what doesn't need to be compromised, and make space to understand what you truly want.

SEX LANGUAGE QUESTIONNAIRE

The Sex Language Questionnaire is designed to assess your kinks and sexual proclivities, determining how you approach foreplay, arousal, the sexual act, and sexual release.

To score, rank each comment on a scale from 1 to 5, with 1 being "definitely disagree," 3 being "neutral," and 5 being "definitely agree." Your highest score is your sex language.

SEXUAL PRAGMATIC

- Sex is more than penetration; it requires preparation.
- I have particular kinks that help me become and stay aroused.
- I believe most sexual activities should include toys.
- I do not believe in conventional sex and prefer complicated positions.
- I want a partner who shares similar fetishes with me.

SEXUAL DRAMATIC

- Intense emotions make me want to take my clothes off
- A significant argument should always follow good sex
- Ripping clothes off is better than taking clothes off
- Spontaneous sex excites me more than planned sex
- Sex becomes more enjoyable when something in the room is damaged as a result of the activity.

SEXUAL PLEASER

- Sex MUST not end until my partner reaches orgasm
- Most times, I would rather please than be pleased
- I am confident in my ability to satisfy my partner sexually, no matter what.
- I feel stressed and unwanted when my partner cannot orgasm.
- I sometimes cannot orgasm if my partner does not orgasm first.

SEXUAL STRAIGHTSHOOTER

- There is no sex without penetration
- Foreplay and the use of toys are somewhat of a waste of time.
- I prefer planning sexual encounters over spontaneous sex.
- I do not have more than three preferred sex positions.
- Sex should be about the destination, not the journey.

SEXUAL CROCKPOTTER

- Sex is about the journey, not the destination
- Foreplay should begin long before penetration occurs
- Sensual seduction is a necessary part of sex
- I like to tease for long periods until my partner can no longer take it
- I like to try different things to crank up the sexual energy

ADVERSE RELATIONSHIP EXPERIENCE SURVEY

The Adverse Relationship Experience Survey is designed to help you understand how severe your past relationships may have affected you. It consists of twenty questions with a Y/N. The higher your score, the higher the likelihood of relational trauma.

Trauma is relative for those experiencing it. You may have a high score and still not show any symptoms of trauma. If you do have symptoms of trauma, please seek guidance from a mental health professional about the next steps.

A. Did an ex-partner **sometimes** or **repeatedly** shove, hit, grab, or bite you out of anger? Y/N

B. Did an ex-partner **sometimes** or **repeatedly** demean, insult, overly criticize, or yell profanities that made you question your character? Y/N

C. Did an ex-partner **sometimes** or **repeatedly** force you to engage in any sexual activity you did not consent to? Y/N

D. Did an ex-partner **sometimes** or **repeatedly** engage in the silent treatment, withdrawal of affection, and passive-aggressive avoidance for extended periods as punishment? Y/N

E. Did an ex-partner **sometimes** or **repeatedly** intimidate you with words or actions to control you? Y/N

F. Did an ex-partner **sometimes** or **repeatedly** humiliate you in front of others? Y/N

G. Did an ex-partner **sometimes** or **repeatedly** threaten self-harm if you attempted to leave or break up? Y/N

H. Did an ex-partner **sometimes** or **repeatedly** make attempts to isolate you from friends and/or family? Y/N

I. Did an ex-partner **sometimes** or **repeatedly** engage in substance use that negatively impacted the relationship? Y/N

J. Did an ex-partner **sometimes** or **repeatedly** engage in poor financial choices that severely impacted the household income? Y/N

K. Did an ex-partner **sometimes** or **repeatedly** use your children as leverage for control with threats of loss? Y/N

L. Did an ex-partner **sometimes** or **repeatedly** utilize financial leverage as a means to control? Y/N

M. Did an ex-partner **sometimes** or **repeatedly** engage in multiple sexual affairs despite adverse emotional side effects? Y/N

N. Did an ex-partner **sometimes** or **repeatedly** engage in stalking behaviors post breakup? Y/N

O. Did an ex-partner **sometimes** or **repeatedly** attempt to control your behaviors against your will? Y/N

P. Did an ex-partner ever die suddenly, while in a relationship with you? Y/N

Q. Did an ex-partner ever go through extensive health-related issues that impacted you emotionally, financially, or mentally? Y/N

R. Did an ex-partner attempt suicide due to an extensively diagnosed mental health condition? Y/N

S. Did an ex-partner commit a significant crime that resulted in sudden financial and emotional consequences for you and the family? Y/N

T. Did an ex-partner experience multiple drug or alcohol rehabilitation visits with little to no change? Y/N

NOTES

NOTES

NOTES

NOTES

NOTES

NOTES

NOTES

NOTES

NOTES

NOTES

NOTES

NOTES

NOTES

NOTES

NOTES

NOTES

NOTES

NOTES

NOTES

NOTES

NOTES

NOTES

NOTES